D0283550

This important book addresses an issue many assume resides outside of evangelical concerns: racial reconciliation in America. Reigniting Martin Luther King's challenge to do the hard work of racial justice *now*, the articles in this volume boldly consider what might be done to effectively respond to a still "racialized" country. An overriding theme of fellowship is woven within this timely volume, encouraging the eager reader, evangelical or not, to imagine anew a beloved community of racial inclusion at the looming sunset of the Obama era. In a most brilliant move, this book calls for evangelicals to carry on the spirit of the Civil Rights Movement while expanding its limitations. It acknowledges that changing legislation is but one step toward racial reconciliation for a people with, as W.E.B. DuBois once eloquently put it, "unreconciled strivings" and "warring ideals." This volume offers the Bible as a potent tonic to change and cure the depraved heart regarding racial equality.

DEREK S. HICKS
Assistant Professor
School of Divinity
Wake Forest University

This collection of personal narratives by gifted Christian leaders—black and white—strikes a blow against indifference to racism and advances the cause of Christ-exalting diversity in the church. *Letters to a Birmingham Jail* looks forward as well as back, addressing the ethnic conflicts of a new generation. It does not seek answers from culture but from the gospel, which transforms both our vertical relationship (with God) and our horizontal relationships (with one another).

DR. PHILIP G. RYKEN
President
Wheaton College

If it were within my means, I'd buy 100,000 copies of *Letters to a Birmingham Jail* and give them away to pastors and Christians all across America. This book is just that important to the future of Christianity in America. Be warned, though: the borders of your present reality will breached by the flood of truth that overflows out of every page. You will be called into a deeper, more beautiful, gospel story that births missional, gospel-centered, multi-ethnic churches.

> DERWIN L. GRAY
> *Lead Pastor Transformation Church*
> *Author of* Limitless Life: You Are More Than Your
> Past When God Holds Your Future

Letters to a Birmingham Jail provides a thermostatic rather than a thermometeristic approach to the church's response to inequity and injustice within the world—it serves to adjust rather than to acknowledge the social temperature. It is bathed in a Christo-conciliatory solution that fosters authentic racial reconciliation within the church, thus serving as a headlight rather than a taillight to the world. This book advocates gospelizing the social—that is letting the gospel subversively address the social problems within our world rather than socializing the gospel—making the gospel subservient to the social methodologies employed to address the problems within our world. The soil of this volume carries within it the seeds of the ministry of Jesus that must be cultivated if the church is to lead the way to a true and biblical revolution that engages this world's dilemma. I enthusiastically endorse this work.

> DR. ROBERT SMITH
> *Professor of Divinity*
> *Samford University*

Bryan Loritts has assembled a wonderful group of ethnically diverse church leaders to respond to the now famous letter from the pen of Martin Luther King Jr., which, though written from a Birmingham jail in 1963, continues to appear timeless and relevant today. In response to King's well-known letter, these influential leaders seek to advance the issues raised in that letter by addressing both the vertical and horizontal dimensions of themes such as gospel, church, race, diversity, and racial reconciliation. Each chapter in the volume offers insightful guidance, providing a beautifully harmonized chorus that will challenge readers to think, live, and serve Christianly in a more faithful way in whatever context they may find themselves. The result is a powerful, probing, prophetic, convicting, biblically grounded, gospel-centered, culturally sensitive, interculturally competent, illuminating, helpful, and hopeful book, which I gladly and heartily recommend.

DAVID S. DOCKERY
President
Union University

In the spirit of King's iconic Letter fifty years ago, *Letters to a Birmingham Jail* calls us to contend with the slow, hard work of building a Christ-centered church—one that challenges us to do continual battle with the earthly divisions that diminish all who profess the name of Christ. This book is essential reading.

CHARLES W. MCKINNEY, JR.
Associate Professor of History
Director, African American Studies
Rhodes College

LETTERS TO A BIRMINGHAM JAIL:

A Response to the Words and Dreams
of Dr. Martin Luther King, Jr.

Edited by
BRYAN LORITTS

Moody Publishers

CHICAGO

Published in association with the literary agency of Wolgemuth & Associates, Inc.

Edited by Karen L. Waddles
Interior design: Ragont Design
Cover design: Jason Gabbert Design, LLC
Cover photo: Martin Luther King press conference, *U.S. News & World Report* Magazine Photograph Collection, Prints & Photographs Division, LOC, LC-DIG-ppmsc-01269

Library of Congress Cataloging-in-Publication Data
Letters to a Birmingham jail : a response to the words and dreams of Martin Luther King, Jr. / Bryan Loritts, general editor.
    pages cm
Includes bibliographical references.
ISBN 978-0-8024-1196-9
1. Social justice—United States—Religious aspects--Christianity. 2. Cultural pluralism—United States—Religious aspects—Christianity. 3. Multiculturalism— United States—Religious aspects—Christianity 4. King, Martin Luther, Jr., 1929-1968. Letter from Birmingham jail. 5. Church and minorities—United States. 6. Christian sociology—United States. 7. Christianity and politics—United States. 8. United States—Race relations. 9. United States—Ethnic relations. 10. United States—Religion. I. Loritts, Bryan C., editor of compilation.
BR115.J8L48 2014
261.80973--dc23

                                                    2014002550

We hope you enjoy this book from Moody Publishers. Our goal is to provide high-quality, thought-provoking books and products that connect truth to your real needs and challenges. For more information on other books and products written and produced from a biblical perspective, go to www.moodypublishers.com or write to:

Moody Publishers
820 N. LaSalle Boulevard
Chicago, IL 60610

5 7 9 10 8 6 4

Printed in the United States of America

To Monday Mornings:

McLean, Wilson, Michael, Sam, and Will,
you've been God's hands of healing in my pursuit
of Christ-exalting diversity

To Dr. Martin Luther King Jr.:

Thanks for your redemptive impatience

CONTENTS

FOREWORD

BRYAN LORITTS HAS recruited a serious lineup of pastors, Bible teachers, and Christian senior statesmen to do something that might seem foolish. He has asked them to write letters to the late Dr. Martin Luther King Jr. in response to his famous "Letter from a Birmingham Jail." Dr. King wrote that letter to the white Protestant clergymen of Birmingham, Alabama, in April 1963. They had expressed measured approval of civil rights in principle, but had also cautioned King and his associates about moving too fast or becoming too radical in pursuit of their goals. King responded with a classic statement defending the moral—indeed, the biblical—imperative for full civil equality for black Americans, and for obtaining that equality NOW.

But that, a reasonable person might say, was fifty years ago. Why should Bryan Loritts and his collaborators bring up the subject now? Almost no American in the early twenty-first century objects to laws mandating desegregation. Almost no one believes Jim Crow was right. Almost everyone thinks that equal opportunity under the law is a good and proper thing.

Besides, did not the election of Barack Obama as the United States' first African American president mark an important turning point in the nation's history? Since he took office in January 2009, opponents of Obama have mostly criticized his policies, while his supporters have mostly defended those policies. Except for a tiny fringe of the populace, the president's ethnicity has been almost a nonfactor. Moreover, in the United States' recent past, other political controversies and economic problems have dominated public attention.

Yet for historians and Bible believers alike, there is in fact a great deal more to be said. Quite a few historians, including myself, believe that many of the most important events in American history have involved race in conjunction with religion. Quite a few Bible believers, including the authors in this volume, believe that the explicitly Christian struggle against racism remains to be won.

Looked at from a strictly historical angle, the United States continues to reap great evils from the seed that was sown through centuries of slavery and a century of segregation. Yet guided by candidates eager to be elected and enabled by pundits eager to be heard, we Americans mostly ignore an alarming set of immense social problems.

Whether by comparison with other Western democracies, or even by comparison with many countries in the so-called developing world, the American social order is riven with pathologies. These pathologies have arisen from many factors, but the nation's racial history is everywhere prime among those factors. Here is a short list: the United States has by far the highest rates of incarceration in the Western world; it witnesses more gun violence than any other so-called civilized country; its entertainment industry glorifies violence, misogyny, sexual promiscuity, and infantile self-indulgence; it offers less medical and family support for the poor than any other Western nation; it maintains inequalities of wealth on a par with the kleptocracies of the Third World; its rate of infant mortality is several times higher than most western countries; and, most grievously, the nation is witnessing a disastrous collapse of the two-parent family as the accepted norm for giving birth and raising children. The US racial history is not solely responsible for these indices of social pathology but that history has contributed substantially to every one of them.

Even more, most of us believers need to confess that at least some of the time and in some of our actions, we actively or passively nurture some of the underlying prejudice, paternalism, or attitudes that remain from our country's racist past.

Christian believers who view race and religion as defining the deepest moral failing in American history should be very concerned about heeding the Scriptures that we say we trust, as we approach questions of black-white racial reconciliation. In dynamic fashion, this book outlines the continuing scope of the problem. It also points to the proper medicine for our disease—deeper commitment to the biblical message that in Christ the walls of prejudice that divide people from people have been broken down once and for all.

This is a book that, in its own way, is as timely as the letter that Martin Luther King Jr. wrote fifty years ago.

MARK A. NOLL
Professor of History, University of Notre Dame
Member, South Bend Christian Reformed Church
December 2013

INTRODUCTION

IN THE SPRING OF 1963, Dr. Martin Luther King Jr. and his lieutenants lifted their gaze to what King would later refer to in Messianic terms as his own Golgotha: Birmingham, Alabama. Dr. King's entrance into the city affectionately referred to as "Bombingham" provoked polarizing responses. One can see Commissioner Bull Connor rubbing his hands together poised to unleash his K-9 patrol on passively disobedient marchers. However there was a contingency of clergy who longed for King to exercise patience, after all the old political guard was on its way out, or so the argument went. So this latter group representing various churches and faiths composed a letter imploring Dr. King to let things work themselves out, to not stir up any trouble. They wanted Dr. King to be passive.

King's response to his pensive colleagues became not only history, but his prison epistle would bequeath to us the transcript of his and the movements heart. Over the years many have memorized King's *Letter From a Birmingham Jail*, while countless others would find from it inspiration and sustenance to endure their own Golgotha. But like most historical moments, no one knew what they had in their hands the moment they held it. I guess this would be the only reasonable explanation as to why King's Letter was not published until a full two months after its writing, only in the "afterglow" of Birmingham.[1]

But there's another historical significance to this magnum opus of the civil right's movement. May I suggest that placed in its historical setting, King's passion reveals that Bull Connor was not the only antagonist to the epic drama that was unfolding in the streets of Birmingham

15

in 1963. Locking arms with Commissioner Connor was an enemy so subtle he appeared to be on his side; it was the enemy of indifference. What ignited Dr. King's ire, setting him on a frantic quest for scraps of paper to codify his thoughts, was the passive indifference of clergy beckoning him to wait.

It was Abraham Joshua Heschel, a Jewish rabbi who marched with Dr. King, who told us that the only thing worse than the evil of hatred is indifference. If this be the case, then the movement's most vicious antagonists were not the policemen wielding billy clubs in the streets of Birmingham, but the clergy inviting Dr. King to join their crusade of passive indifference. Lukewarm indifference is a greater threat than white-hot hatred. Just ask the fabled frog in the kettle who became quite intimate with lukewarm. Was this not the very issue Jesus addressed through His exiled apostle John as he delivered a message to the lukewarm Laodicean's? Middle of the road indifference, Jesus said, makes Him sick.

It is this brand of passive racism that continues to pose a serious threat to us experiencing the eclectic community that Dr. King envisioned.

Some years ago I was on a subway in New York City enjoying a good conversation with a friend of mine, when I noticed something peculiar. Every time the train stopped he would close his eyes mid conversation while people boarded. After a few stops I couldn't hold my peace. I asked him why he closed his eyes every time our train stopped. Embarrassed, he reflected on how his mother had raised him, that if he was ever in a situation where there were no seats and women were standing, the chivalrous thing to do would be to give up his seat. He didn't want to do that on this day; so he reasoned that if he would just close his eyes and not see women standing, he could continue his comfortable life.

Who hasn't found themselves doing something similar? I know I have. Some have closed their eyes to the poor, others to the educational injustice and economic disparities that continue to plague our country. And, yes, some continue to close their eyes, not wanting to do the hard work of going to the other part of town getting to know someone who doesn't think like, act like, look like, or vote like me. Far too many of us know the temptation to close our eyes.

CHRIST-EXALTING DIVERSITY

The death of Jesus Christ on a lonely Friday afternoon in Jerusalem was the intentional, aggressive, costly initiative of God to adopt into His family people from every nation, tribe, and tongue. Jesus did not cover His eyes in the hopes that He would not feel obligated to leave His seat in heaven. Instead, He looked upon us standing sinners, and intentionally gave up His comfortable seat, embracing the discomfort of the cross so that we might sit and reign with Him for all eternity. The brutal death of Jesus negates any notion of our salvation coming by passive means.

If our vertical reconciliation to God required intentionality, then our horizontal reconciliation necessitates the same intentionality. Dr. King's slain corpse on the balcony of the Lorraine Motel on that April day in 1968 is a fitting image of the costly nature of reconciliation; and it is for this reason that we write this book. What you hold in your hands is our attempt to inspire people to not cover their eyes in passivity, but to pursue Christ-exalting diversity.

BRYAN LORITTS
Memphis, Tennessee

Letter from a Birmingham Jail

April 16, 1963

My Dear Fellow Clergymen:

While confined here in the Birmingham City Jail, I came across your recent statement calling my present activities "unwise and untimely." Seldom do I pause to answer criticism of my work and ideas. If I sought to answer all the criticisms that cross my desk, my secretaries would have little time for anything other than such correspondence in the course of the day, and I would have no time for constructive work. But since I feel that you are men of genuine goodwill and that your criticisms are sincerely set forth, I want to try to answer your statements in what I hope will be patient and reasonable terms.

I think I should indicate why I am here in Birmingham, since you have been influenced by the view which argues against "outsiders coming in." I have the honor of serving as president of the Southern Christian Leadership Conference, an organization operating in every Southern state, with headquarters in Atlanta, Georgia. We have some eighty-five affiliated organizations across the South, and one of them is the Alabama Christian Movement for Human Rights. Frequently we share staff, educational, and financial resources with our affiliates. Several months ago the affiliate here in Birmingham asked us to be on call to engage in a non-violent direct-action program if such were deemed necessary. We readily consented, and when the hour came we lived up to our promise. So I, along with several members of my staff, am here because I was invited here. I am here because I have organizational ties here.

But more basically, I am in Birmingham because injustice is here. Just as the prophets of the eighth century B.C. left their villages and carried their "thus saith the Lord" far beyond the boundaries of their hometowns, and just as the Apostle Paul left his village of Tarsus and carried the gospel of Jesus Christ to the far corners of the Greco-Roman world, so am I compelled to carry the gospel of freedom far beyond my own hometown. Like Paul, I must constantly respond to the Macedonian call for aid.

Moreover, I am cognizant of the interrelatedness of all communities and states. I cannot sit idly by in Atlanta and not be concerned about what happens in Birmingham. Injustice anywhere is a threat to justice everywhere. We are caught in an inescapable network of mutuality, tied in a single garment of destiny. Whatever affects one directly, affects all indirectly. Never again can we afford to live with the narrow, provincial "outside agitator" idea. Anyone who lives inside the United States can never be considered an outsider anywhere within its bounds.

You deplore the demonstrations taking place in Birmingham. But your statement, I am sorry to say, fails to express a similar concern for the conditions that brought about the demonstrations. I am sure that none of you would want to rest content with the superficial kind of social analysis that deals merely with effects and does not grapple with underlying causes. It is unfortunate that demonstrations are taking place in Birmingham, but it is even more unfortunate that the city's white power structure left the Negro community with no alternative.

In any nonviolent campaign there are four basic steps: collection of the facts to determine whether injustices exist; negotiation; self-purification; and direct action. We have gone through all of these steps in Birmingham. There can be no gainsaying the fact that racial injustice engulfs this community. Birmingham is probably the most thoroughly segregated city in the United States. Its ugly record of brutality is widely known. Negroes have experienced grossly unjust treatment in the courts. There have been more unsolved bombings of Negro homes and churches in Birmingham than in any other city in the nation. These are the hard, brutal facts of the case. On the basis of these conditions, Negro leaders sought to negotiate with the city fathers. But the latter consistently refused to engage in good-faith negotiation.

Then, last September, came the opportunity to talk with leaders of Birmingham's economic community. In the course of the negotiations, certain promises were made by the merchants—for example, to remove the stores' humiliating racial signs. On the basis of these promises, the Reverend Fred Shuttlesworth and the leaders of the Alabama Christian Movement for Human Rights agreed to a moratorium on all demonstrations. As the weeks and months went by, we realized that we were the victims of a broken promise. A few signs, briefly removed, returned; the others remained.

As in so many past experiences, our hopes had been blasted, and the shadow of deep disappointment settled upon us. We had no alternative except to prepare for direct action, whereby we would present our very bodies as a means of laying our case before the conscience of the local and the national community. Mindful of the difficulties involved, we decided to undertake a process of self-purification. We began a series of workshops on nonviolence, and we repeatedly asked ourselves: "Are you able to accept blows without retaliating?" "Are you able to endure the ordeal of jail?" We decided to schedule our direct-action program for the Easter season, realizing that except for Christmas, this is the main shopping period of the year. Knowing that a strong economic withdrawal program would be the byproduct of direct action, we felt that this would be the best time to bring pressure to bear on the merchants for the needed change.

Then it occurred to us that Birmingham's mayoralty election was coming up in March, and we speedily decided to postpone action until after Election Day. When we discovered that the Commissioner of Police

Safety, Eugene "Bull" Connor, had piled up enough votes to be in the run-off, we decided again to postpone action until the day after the run-off so that the demonstrations could not be used to cloud the issues. Like many others, we waited to see Mr. Connor defeated, and to this end we endured postponement after postponement. Having aided in this community need, we felt that our direct-action program could be delayed no longer.

You may well ask: "Why direct action? Why sit-ins, marches and so forth? Isn't negotiation a better path?" You are quite right in calling for negotiation. Indeed, this is the very purpose of direct action. Nonviolent direct action seeks to create such a crisis and foster such a tension that a community which has constantly refused to negotiate is forced to confront the issue. It seeks to so dramatize the issue that it can no longer be ignored. My citing the creation of tension as part of the work of the nonviolent-resister may sound rather shocking. But I must confess that I am not afraid of the word "tension." I have earnestly opposed violent tension, but there is a type of constructive, nonviolent tension which is necessary for growth. Just as Socrates felt that it was necessary to create a tension in the mind so that individuals could rise from the bondage of myths and half-truths to the unfettered realm of creative analysis and objective appraisal, so must we see the need for nonviolent gadflies to create the kind of tension in society that will help men rise from the dark depths of prejudice and racism to the majestic heights of understanding and brotherhood.

The purpose of our direct-action program is to create a situation so crisis-packed that it will inevitably open the door to negotiation. I therefore concur with you in your call for negotiation. Too long has our beloved Southland been bogged down in a tragic effort to live in monologue rather than dialogue.

One of the basic points in your statement is that the action that I and my associates have taken in Birmingham is untimely. Some have asked: "Why didn't you give the new city administration time to act?" The only answer that I can give to this query is that the new Birmingham administration must be prodded about as much as the outgoing one, before it will act. We are sadly mistaken if we feel that the election of Albert Boutwell as mayor will bring the millennium to Birmingham. While Mr. Boutwell is a much more gentle person than Mr. Connor, they are both segregationists, dedicated to maintenance of the status quo. I have hope that Mr. Boutwell will be reasonable enough to see the futility of massive resistance to desegregation. But he will not see this without pressure from devotees of civil rights. My friends, I must say to you that we have not made a single gain in civil rights without determined legal and nonviolent pressure.

Lamentably, it is an historical fact that privileged groups seldom give up their privileges voluntarily. Individuals may see the moral light and voluntarily give up their unjust posture; but, as Reinhold Niebuhr has reminded us, groups tend to be more immoral than individuals.

We know through painful experience that freedom is never voluntarily given by the oppressor; it must be demanded by the oppressed. Frankly, I have yet to engage in a direct-action campaign that was "well timed" in the view of those who have not suffered unduly from the disease of segregation. For years now I have heard the word "Wait!" It rings in the ear of every Negro with piercing familiarity. This "Wait" has almost always meant "Never." We must come to see, with one of our distinguished jurists, that "justice too long delayed is justice denied."

We have waited for more than 340 years for our constitutional and God-given rights. The nations of Asia and Africa are moving with jetlike speed toward gaining political independence, but we still creep at horse-

and-buggy pace toward gaining a cup of coffee at a lunch counter.

Perhaps it is easy for those who have never felt the stinging darts of segregation to say, "Wait." But when you have seen vicious mobs lynch your mothers and fathers at will and drown your sisters and brothers at whim; when you have seen hate-filled policemen curse, kick and even kill your black brothers and sisters; when you see the vast majority of your twenty million Negro brothers smothering in an airtight cage of poverty in the midst of an affluent society; when you suddenly find your tongue twisted and your speech stammering as you seek to explain to your six-year-old daughter why she can't go to the public amusement park that has just been advertised on television, and see tears welling up in her eyes when she is told that Funtown is closed to colored children, and see ominous clouds of inferiority beginning to form in her little mental sky, and see her beginning to distort her personality by developing an unconscious bitterness toward white people; when you have to concoct an answer for a five-year-old son who is asking: "Daddy, why do white people treat colored people so mean?"; when you take a cross-country drive and find it necessary to sleep night after night in the uncomfortable corners of your automobile because no motel will accept you; when you are humiliated day in and day out by nagging signs reading "white" and "colored"; when your first name becomes "nigger," your middle name becomes "boy" (however old you are) and your last name becomes "John," and your wife and mother are never given the respected title "Mrs."; when you are harried by day and haunted by night by the fact that you are a Negro, living constantly at tiptoe stance, never quite knowing what to expect next, and are plagued with inner fears and outer resentments; when you go forever fighting a degenerating sense of "nobodiness"— then you will understand why we find it difficult to wait. There comes a time when the cup of endurance runs over, and men are no longer willing to be plunged into the abyss of despair. I hope, sirs, you can understand our legitimate and unavoidable impatience.

You express a great deal of anxiety over our willingness to break laws. This is certainly a legitimate concern. Since we so diligently urge people to obey the Supreme Court's decision of 1954 outlawing segregation in the public schools, at first glance it may seem rather paradoxical for us consciously to break laws. One may well ask: "How can you advocate breaking some laws and obeying others?" The answer lies in the fact that there are two types of laws: just and unjust. I would be the first to advocate obeying just laws. One has not only a legal but a moral responsibility to obey just laws. Conversely, one has a moral responsibility to disobey unjust laws. I would agree with St. Augustine that "an unjust law is no law at all."

Now, what is the difference between the two? How does one determine whether a law is just or unjust? A just law is a man-made code that squares with the moral law or the law of God. An unjust law is a code that is out of harmony with the moral law. To put it in the terms of St. Thomas Aquinas: An unjust law is a human law that is not rooted in eternal law and natural law. Any law that uplifts human personality is just. Any law that degrades human personality is unjust. All segregation statutes are unjust because segregation distorts the soul and damages the personality. It gives the segregator a false sense of superiority and the segregated a false sense of inferiority. Segregation, to use the terminology of the Jewish philosopher Martin Buber, substitutes an "I-it" relationship for an "I-thou" relationship and ends up relegating persons to the status of things. Hence segregation is not only politically, economically, and sociologically unsound, it is morally wrong and awful. Paul Tillich has said that sin is separation. Is not segregation an existential expression of man's tragic separation, his awful estrangement, his terrible sinfulness? Thus it is that I can urge men to obey the 1954 decision of the Supreme Court, for it is morally right; and I can urge them to disobey segregation ordinances, for they are morally wrong.

Let us consider a more concrete example of just and unjust laws. An unjust law is a code that a numerical or power majority group compels a minority group to obey but does not make binding on itself. This is *difference* made legal. By the same token, a just law is a code that a majority compels a minority to follow and that it is willing to follow itself. This is *sameness* made legal.

Let me give another explanation. A law is unjust if it is inflicted on a minority that, as a result of being denied the right to vote, had no part in enacting or devising the law. Who can say that the legislature of Alabama which set up that state's segregation laws was democratically elected? Throughout Alabama all sorts of devious methods are used to prevent Negroes from becoming registered voters, and there are some counties in which, even though Negroes constitute a majority of the population, not a single Negro is registered. Can any law enacted under such circumstances be considered democratically structured?

Sometimes a law is just on its face and unjust in its application. For instance, I have been arrested on a charge of parading without a permit. Now, there is nothing wrong in having an ordinance which requires a permit for a parade. But such an ordinance becomes unjust when it is used to maintain segregation and to deny citizens the First Amendment privilege of peaceful assembly and protest.

I hope you are able to see the distinction I am trying to point out. In no sense do I advocate evading or defying the law, as would the rabid segregationist. That would lead to anarchy. One who breaks an unjust law must do so openly, lovingly, and with a willingness to accept the penalty. I submit that an individual who breaks a law that conscience tells him is unjust. and who willingly accepts the penalty of imprisonment in order to arouse the conscience of the community over its injustice, is in reality expressing the highest respect for law.

Of course, there is nothing new about this kind of civil disobedience. It was evidenced sublimely in the refusal of Shadrach, Meshach, and Abednego to obey the laws of Nebuchadnezzar, on the ground that a higher moral law was at stake. It was practiced superbly by the early Christians, who were willing to face hungry lions and the excruciating pain of chopping blocks rather than submit to certain unjust laws of the Roman Empire. To a degree, academic freedom is a reality today because Socrates practiced civil disobedience. In our own nation, the Boston Tea Party represented a massive act of civil disobedience.

We should never forget that everything Adolf Hitler did in Germany was "legal" and everything the Hungarian freedom fighters did in Hungary was "illegal." It was "illegal" to aid and comfort a Jew in Hitler's Germany. Even so, I am sure that, had I lived in Germany at the time, I would have aided and comforted my Jewish brothers. If today I lived in a Communist country where certain principles dear to the Christian faith are suppressed, I would openly advocate disobeying that country's anti-religious laws.

I must make two honest confessions to you, my Christian and Jewish brothers. First, I must confess that over the past few years I have been gravely disappointed with the white moderate. I have almost reached the regrettable conclusion that the Negro's great stumbling block in his stride toward freedom is not the White Citizen's Counciler or the Ku Klux Klanner, but the white moderate, who is more devoted to "order" than to justice; who prefers a negative peace which is the absence of tension to a positive peace which is the presence of justice; who constantly says: "I agree with you in the goal you seek, but I cannot agree with your methods of direct action"; who paternalistically believes he can set the timetable for another man's freedom; who lives by a mythical concept of time and who constantly advises the Negro to wait for a "more convenient season." Shallow understanding from people of good will is more frustrating than absolute misunderstanding from people of ill will. Lukewarm acceptance is much more bewildering than outright rejection.

I had hoped that the white moderate would understand that law and order exist for the purpose of establishing justice and that when they fail in this purpose they become the dangerously structured dams that block the flow of social progress. I had hoped that the white moderate would understand that the present tension in the South is a necessary phase of the transition from an obnoxious negative peace, in which the Negro passively accepted his unjust plight, to a substantive and positive peace, in which all men will respect the dignity and worth of human personality. Actually, we who engage in nonviolent direct action are not the creators of tension. We merely bring to the surface the hidden tension that is already alive. We bring it out in the open, where it can be seen and dealt with. Like a boil that can never be cured so long as it is covered up but must be opened, with all its ugliness, to the natural medicines of air and light, injustice must be exposed, with all the tension its exposure creates, to the light of human conscience and the air of national opinion before it can be cured.

In your statement you assert that our actions, even though peaceful, must be condemned because they precipitate violence. But is this a logical assertion? Isn't this like condemning a robbed man because his possession of money precipitated the evil act of robbery? Isn't this like condemning Socrates because his unswerving commitment to truth and his philosophical inquiries precipitated the act by the misguided populace in which they made him drink hemlock? Isn't this like condemning

Jesus because his unique God-consciousness and never-ceasing devotion to God's will precipitated the evil act of crucifixion? We must come to see that, as the federal courts have consistently affirmed, it is wrong to urge an individual to cease his efforts to gain his basic constitutional rights because the quest may precipitate violence. Society must protect the robbed and punish the robber.

I had also hoped that the white moderate would reject the myth concerning time in relation to the struggle for freedom. I have just received a letter from a white brother in Texas. He writes: "All Christians know that the colored people will receive equal rights eventually, but it is possible that you are in too great a religious hurry. It has taken Christianity almost two thousand years to accomplish what it has. The teachings of Christ take time to come to earth." Such an attitude stems from a tragic misconception of time, from the strangely rational notion that there is something in the very flow of time that will inevitably cure all ills. Actually, time itself is neutral; it can be used either destructively or constructively. More and more I feel that the people of ill will have used time much more effectively than have the people of good will. We will have to repent in this generation not merely for the hateful words and actions of the bad people but for the appalling silence of the good people. Human progress never rolls in on wheels of inevitability; it comes through the tireless efforts of men willing to be co-workers with God, and without this hard work, time itself becomes an ally of the forces of social stagnation. We must use time creatively, in the knowledge that the time is always ripe to do right. Now is the time to make real the promise of democracy and transform our pending national elegy into a creative psalm of brotherhood. Now is the time to lift our national policy from the quicksand of racial injustice to the solid rock of human dignity.

You speak of our activity in Birmingham as extreme. At first I was rather disappointed that fellow clergymen would see my nonviolent efforts as those of an extremist. I began thinking about the fact that I stand in the middle of two opposing forces in the Negro community. One is a force of complacency, made up in part of Negroes who, as a result of long years of oppression, are so drained of self-respect and a sense of "somebodiness" that they have adjusted to segregation; and in part of a few middle class Negroes who, because of a degree of academic and economic security and because in some ways they profit by segregation, have become insensitive to the problems of the masses. The other force is one of bitterness and hatred, and it comes perilously close to advocating violence. It is expressed in the various black nationalist groups that are springing up across the nation, the largest and best-known being Elijah Muhammad's Muslim movement. Nourished by the Negro's frustration over the continued existence of racial discrimination, this movement is made up of people who have lost faith in America, who have absolutely repudiated Christianity, and who have concluded that the white man is an incorrigible "devil."

I have tried to stand between these two forces, saying that we need emulate neither the "do-nothingism" of the complacent nor the hatred and despair of the black nationalist. For there is the more excellent way of love and nonviolent protest. I am grateful to God that, through the influence of the Negro church, the way of nonviolence became an integral part of our struggle.

If this philosophy had not emerged, by now many streets of the South would, I am convinced, be flowing with blood. And I am further convinced that if our white brothers dismiss as "rabble-rousers" and "outside agitators" those of us who employ nonviolent direct action, and if they refuse to support our nonviolent efforts, millions of Negroes will, out of frustration and despair, seek solace and security in black-nationalist ideologies—a development that would inevitably lead to a frightening racial nightmare.

Oppressed people cannot remain oppressed forever. The yearning for freedom eventually manifests itself, and that is what has happened to the American Negro. Something within has reminded him of his birthright of freedom; and something without has reminded him that it can be gained. Consciously or unconsciously, he has been caught up by the *Zeitgeist,* and with his black brothers of Africa and his brown and yellow brothers of Asia, South America, and the Caribbean, the United States Negro is moving with a sense of great urgency toward the promised land of racial justice. If one recognizes this vital urge that has engulfed the Negro community, one should readily understand why public demonstrations are taking place. The Negro has many pent-up resentments and latent frustrations, and he must release them. So let him march; let him make prayer pilgrimages to the city hall; let him go on freedom rides—and try to understand why he must do so. If his repressed emotions are not released in nonviolent ways, they will seek expression through violence; this is not a threat but a fact of history. So I have not said to my people: "Get rid of your discontent." Rather, I have tried to say that this normal and healthy discontent can be channeled into the creative outlet of nonviolent direct action. And now this approach is being termed extremist.

But though I was initially disappointed at being categorized as an extremist, as I continued to think about the matter I gradually gained a measure of satisfaction from the label. Was not Jesus an extremist for love: "Love your enemies, bless them that curse you, do good to them that hate you, and pray for them which despitefully use you, and persecute you." Was not Amos an extremist for justice: "Let justice roll down like waters and righteousness like an ever-flowing stream." Was not Paul

31

an extremist for the Christian gospel: "I bear in my body the marks of the Lord Jesus." Was not Martin Luther an extremist: "Here I stand; I cannot do otherwise, so help me God." And John Bunyan: "I will stay in jail to the end of my days before I make a butchery of my conscience." And Abraham Lincoln: "This nation cannot survive half slave and half free." And Thomas Jefferson: "We hold these truths to be self-evident, that all men are created equal . . . " So the question is not whether we will be extremists, but what kind of extremists we will be. Will we be extremists for hate or for love? Will we be extremists for the preservation of injustice or for the extension of justice? In that dramatic scene on Calvary's hill three men were crucified. We must never forget that all three were crucified for the same crime—the crime of extremism. Two were extremists for immorality, and thus fell below their environment. The other, Jesus Christ, was an extremist for love, truth, and goodness, and thereby rose above his environment. Perhaps the South, the nation, and the world are in dire need of creative extremists.

I had hoped that the white moderate would see this need. Perhaps I was too optimistic; perhaps I expected too much. I suppose I should have realized that few members of the oppressor race can understand the deep groans and passionate yearnings of the oppressed race, and still fewer have the vision to see that injustice must be rooted out by strong, persistent, and determined action. I am thankful, however, that some of our white brothers in the South have grasped the meaning of this social revolution and committed themselves to it. They are still too few in quantity, but they are big in quality. Some—such as Ralph McGill, Lillian Smith, Harry Golden, James McBride Dabbs, Ann Braden, and Sarah Patton Boyle—have written about our struggle in eloquent and prophetic terms. Others have marched with us down nameless streets of the South. They have languished in filthy, roach-infested jails, suffering the abuse and brutality of policemen who view them as "dirty nigger-lovers." Unlike so many of their moderate brothers and sisters, they have recognized the urgency of the moment and sensed the need for powerful "action" antidotes to combat the disease of segregation.

Let me take note of my other major disappointment. I have been so greatly disappointed with the white church and its leadership. Of course, there are some notable exceptions. I am not unmindful of the fact that each of you has taken some significant stands on this issue. I commend you, Reverend Stallings, for your Christian stand on this past Sunday, in welcoming Negroes to your worship service on a nonsegregated basis. I commend the Catholic leaders of this state for integrating Spring Hill College several years ago.

But despite these notable exceptions, I must honestly reiterate that I have been disappointed with the church. I do not say this as one of those negative critics who can always find something wrong with the church. I say this as a minister of the gospel, who loves the church; who was nurtured in its bosom; who has been sustained by its spiritual blessings and who will remain true to it as long as the cord of life shall lengthen.

When I was suddenly catapulted into the leadership of the bus protest in Montgomery, Alabama, a few years ago, I felt we would be supported by the white church. I felt that the white ministers, priests, and rabbis of the South would be among our strongest allies. Instead, some have been outright opponents, refusing to understand the freedom movement and misrepresenting its leaders; all too many others have been more cautious than courageous and have remained silent behind the anesthetizing security of stained-glass windows.

In spite of my shattered dreams, I came to Birmingham with the hope that the white religious leadership of this community would see the justice of our cause and, with deep moral concern, would serve as the channel through which our just grievances could reach the power structure. I had hoped that each of you would understand. But again I have been disappointed.

I have heard numerous southern religious leaders admonish their worshipers to comply with a desegregation decision because it is the law, but I have longed to hear white ministers declare: "Follow this decree because integration is morally right and because the Negro is your brother." In the midst of blatant injustices inflicted upon the Negro, I have watched white churchmen stand on the sideline and mouth pious irrelevancies and sanctimonious trivialities. In the midst of a mighty struggle to rid our nation of racial and economic injustice, I have heard many ministers say: "Those are social issues, with which the gospel has no real concern." And I have watched many churches commit themselves to a completely other-worldly religion which makes a strange, un-Biblical distinction between body and soul, between the sacred and the secular.

I have traveled the length and breadth of Alabama, Mississippi, and all the other southern states. On sweltering summer days and crisp autumn mornings I have looked at the South's beautiful churches with their lofty spires pointing heavenward. I have beheld the impressive outlines of her massive religious-education buildings. Over and over I have found myself asking: "What kind of people worship here? Who is their God? Where were their voices when the lips of Governor Barnett dripped with words of interposition and nullification? Where were they when Governor Wallace gave a clarion call for defiance and hatred? Where were their voices of support when bruised and weary Negro men and women decided to rise from the dark dungeons of complacency to the bright hills of creative protest?"

Yes, these questions are still in my mind. In deep disappointment I have wept over the laxity of the church. But be assured that my tears have been tears of love. There can be no deep disappointment where there is not deep love. Yes, I love the church. How could I do otherwise? I am in the rather unique position of being the son, the grandson, and the great-grandson of preachers. Yes, I see the church as the body of Christ. But, oh! How we have blemished and scarred that body through social neglect and through fear of being nonconformists.

There was a time when the church was very powerful—in the time when the early Christians rejoiced at being deemed worthy to suffer for what they believed. In those days the church was not merely a thermometer that recorded the ideas and principles of popular opinion; it was a thermostat that transformed the mores of society. Whenever the early Christians entered a town, the people in power became disturbed and immediately sought to convict the Christians for being "disturbers of the peace" and "outside agitators." But the Christians pressed on, in the conviction that they were "a colony of heaven," called to obey God rather than man. Small in number, they were big in commitment. They were too God intoxicated to be "astronomically intimidated." By their effort and example they brought an end to such ancient evils as infanticide and gladiatorial contests.

Things are different now. So often the contemporary church is a weak, ineffectual voice with an uncertain sound. So often it is an arch-defender of the status quo. Far from being disturbed by the presence of the church, the power structure of the average community is consoled by the church's silent—and often even vocal—sanction of things as they are.

But the judgment of God is upon the church as never before. If today's church does not recapture the sacrificial spirit of the early church, it will lose its authenticity, forfeit the loyalty of millions, and be dismissed as an irrelevant social club with no meaning for the twentieth century.

Every day I meet young people whose disappointment with the church has turned into outright disgust.

Perhaps I have once again been too optimistic. Is organized religion too inextricably bound to the status quo to save our nation and the world? Perhaps I must turn my faith to the inner spiritual church, the church within the church, as the true **_ekklesia_** and the hope of the world. But again I am thankful to God that some noble souls from the ranks of organized religion have broken loose from the paralyzing chains of conformity and joined us as active partners in the struggle for freedom. They have left their secure congregations and walked the streets of Albany, Georgia with us. They have gone down the highways of the South on torturous rides for freedom. Yes, they have gone to jail with us. Some have been dismissed from their churches and have lost the support of their bishops and fellow ministers. But they have acted in the faith that right defeated is stronger than evil triumphant. Their witness has been the spiritual salt that has preserved the true meaning of the gospel in these troubled times. They have carved a tunnel of hope through the dark mountain of disappointment.

I hope the church as a whole will meet the challenge of this decisive hour. But even if the church does not come to the aid of justice, I have no despair about the future. I have no fear about the outcome of our struggle in Birmingham, even if our motives are at present misunderstood. We will reach the goal of freedom in Birmingham and all over the nation, because the goal of America is freedom. Abused and scorned though we may be, our destiny is tied up with America's destiny. Before the pilgrims landed at Plymouth, we were here. Before the pen of Jefferson etched the majestic words of the Declaration of Independence across the pages of history, we were here. For more than two centuries our forebears labored in this country without wages; they made cotton king; they built the homes of their masters while suffering gross injustice and shameful humiliation—and yet out of a bottomless vitality they continued to thrive and develop. If the inexpressible cruelties of slavery could not stop us, the opposition we now face will surely fail. We will win our freedom because the sacred heritage of our nation and the eternal will of God are embodied in our echoing demands.

Before closing I feel impelled to mention one other point in your statement that has troubled me profoundly. You warmly commended the Birmingham police force for keeping "order" and "preventing violence." I doubt that you would have so warmly commended the police force if you had seen its dogs sinking their teeth into unarmed, nonviolent Negroes. I doubt that you would so quickly commend the policemen if you were to observe their ugly and inhumane treatment of Negroes here in the city jail; if you were to watch them push and curse old Negro women and young Negro girls; if you were to see them slap and kick old Negro men and young boys; if you were to observe them, as they did on two occasions, refuse to give us food because we wanted to sing our grace together. I cannot join you in your praise of the Birmingham police department.

It is true that the police have exercised a degree of discipline in handling the demonstrators. In this sense they have conducted themselves rather "nonviolently" in public. But for what purpose? To preserve the evil system of segregation. Over the past few years I have consistently preached that nonviolence demands that the means we use must be as pure as the ends we seek. I have tried to make clear that it is wrong to use immoral means to attain moral ends. But now I must affirm that it is just as wrong, or perhaps even more so, to use moral means to preserve immoral ends. Perhaps Mr. Connor and his policemen have been rather nonviolent in public, as was Chief Pritchett in Albany, Georgia; but they have used the moral means of nonviolence to maintain the immoral end of racial injustice. As T. S. Eliot has said: "The last temptation is the greatest treason: To do the right deed for the wrong reason."

I wish you had commended the Negro sit-inners and demonstrators of Birmingham for their sublime courage, their willingness to suffer, and their amazing discipline in the midst of great provocation. One day the South will recognize its real heroes. There will be the James Merediths, with the noble sense of purpose that enables them to face jeering and hostile mobs, and with the agonizing loneliness that characterizes the life of the pioneer. There will be the old, oppressed, battered Negro women, symbolized in a seventy-two-year-old woman in Montgomery, Alabama, who rose up with a sense of dignity and with her people decided not to ride segregated buses, and who responded with ungrammatical profundity to one who inquired about her weariness: "My feets is tired, but my soul is at rest. "There will be the young high school and college students, the young ministers of the gospel, and a host of their elders, courageously and nonviolently sitting in at lunch counters and willingly going to jail for conscience' sake. One day the South will know that when these disinherited children of God sat down at lunch counters, they were in reality standing up for what is best in the American dream and for the most sacred values in our Judaeo-Christian heritage, thereby bringing our nation back to those great wells of democracy which were dug deep by the founding fathers in their formulation of the Constitution and the Declaration of Independence.

Never before have I written so long a letter. I'm afraid it is much too long to take your precious time. I can assure you that it would have been much shorter if I had been writing from a comfortable desk, but what else can one do when he is alone in a narrow jail cell, other than write long letters, think long thoughts, and pray long prayers?

If I have said anything in this letter that overstates the truth and indicates an unreasonable impatience, I beg you to forgive me. If I have said anything that understates the truth and indicates my having a patience that allows me to settle for anything less than brotherhood, I beg God to forgive me.

I hope this letter finds you strong in the faith. I also hope that circumstances will soon make it possible for me to meet each of you, not as an integrationist or a civil rights leader but as a fellow clergyman and a Christian brother. Let us all hope that the dark clouds of racial prejudice will soon pass away and the deep fog of misunderstanding will be lifted from our fear-drenched communities, and in some not too distant tomorrow the radiant stars of love and brotherhood will shine over our great nation with all their scintillating beauty.

Yours for the cause of Peace and Brotherhood,

Martin Luther King, Jr.

1

WHY WE CAN'T WAIT FOR ECONOMIC JUSTICE

John Perkins

WELL, MARTIN, there've been a few risings and settings of the sun since you wrote your letter from that Birmingham jail. You could not have known what that letter and your death would do to propel the cause of equal rights in this nation. Many of us during that time dared to dream the same dream that you gave words to. And many have paid the ultimate price to see that dream come to fruition. Thank you for giving voice to our struggle. Thank you for trusting in God and serving him in both life and death.

God worked in mysterious ways to prepare my life for engagement with the struggle that you gave your life to and for. His most powerful shaping came in the form of the death of my mother.

I was born in 1930 in New Hebron, Mississippi. My mother died of starvation when I was seven months old. My earliest memory is hearing the words, "Your mother is dead." Even as a young child, I knew that there was something really wrong with a person dying because of the lack of resources to buy food. I suppose this reality set the course of my life—at least subconsciously, Martin—on a track to champion the rights of those who were disenfranchised: the poor.

After my mother's death, the five children in our family, three boys and two girls, were taken in by my grandmother. She had already given birth to and was raising nineteen of her own children. My people were poor sharecroppers. The sharecropping system was an extension of the slave system. For those slaves who did not have land and had been property themselves, the sharecropping system put them back to work on a system that was semislave. It was a hard life. There was no such thing as economic justice for the sharecropper. His survival was dependent on a God-given ability to do much with little—and his willingness to remain silent when he was taken advantage of.

I learned this lesson of survival early in life. When I was about eleven or twelve years old, I worked a whole day hauling hay for a white gentleman. I was expecting to get a dollar or a dollar and a half for that day of work. But at the end of the day, he gave me a dime and a buffalo nickel . . . one dime and one buffalo nickel. What I really wanted to do with it was take it and throw it on the ground, because I had value and worth. My value and my worth were well placed in my labor. I wasn't asking for him to give me anything. So I was completely affronted. It affronted my whole being. That's when I discovered that I had dignity, but I didn't have any way to protect it.

The harsh realities of bigotry and racism stirred the embers of anger and bitterness in my heart. I had not come to know the Lord yet, so this internal storm was raging towards a dangerous end.

My brother Clyde served faithfully in World War II, fighting Hitler's war. He survived the horrors of that war only to be reminded that he still had no rights in this country as a black man. When Clyde was murdered by a white police officer in 1947, I knew that I had to leave Mississippi—to stay would have meant certain death for an angry seventeen-year-old boy. So I went to California to get a fresh start.

California provided an environment far from the glare and oppression of Southern racism. It was the ideal place to start a family, so I married Vera Mae Buckley and was soon drafted to serve two years in the military. After my return from the military, our family began to grow and the first two of our children were born.

Our four-year-old son, Spencer, began attending a church and I was able to see a change in him, as he insisted on quoting a Bible verse before every meal. I went along to hear what he was learning. It was here that I heard the glorious gospel of Jesus Christ preached. The words of Galatians 2:20 (KJV)spoke directly to my heart: *I am crucified with Christ: nevertheless I live; yet not I, but Christ liveth in me: and the life which I now live in the flesh I live by the faith of the Son of God, who loved me, and gave himself for me.* Martin, my life changed at that very moment. I learned that I was loved by a holy God. As I look back on everything, it seems like since that moment I've been carried along by the hand of God.

When I visited a prison in California to share my faith, staring at me from behind the prison bars were young black men who looked just like me. Many of them had come from the Deep South to make a new start, but just didn't make it. As I looked at those young men and interacted with them, I knew God was calling me back to Mississippi. Back to that place of bigotry and racism—there was much that was unfinished in my heart toward Mississippi. There was much that God intended to teach me about His love for people—regardless of color. So at thirty years of age I came back to Mississippi to begin the work that God was calling me to.

In 1963 a group of civil rights workers came and spoke to me about the Voting Rights Drive and we got involved in it. When we heard about all you were doing for the cause, this was an inspiration for our work in voter registration. We got excited about the possibility of One Person—One Vote. This meant recognition of our personhood! It was the affirmation of our dignity as human beings! The Voting Rights Act was the beginning of the end of that old sharecropping system. We helped to organize voters in our county and the surrounding five counties in spite of tremendous threats from the Ku Klux Klan and other organizations that were determined that the Southern system was not going to change.

The great state of Mississippi was not ready yet to yield to the law of the land. It had a system already in place to handle agitators: jail. You found that out in Birmingham, Martin, when you were unjustly arrested. Darkness seemed to have the upper hand. Those must have been some difficult nights for you. But we already knew that great things can happen in jail. They can imprison your body, but they can't imprison your mind.

> **I KNEW THAT IF I didn't forgive, I would be overcome by the same darkness. I purposed at that moment to preach the gospel strong enough to win whites and blacks—to burn through the bigotry and hatred of racism.**

The apostle Paul called himself a prisoner of Christ, and declared that God can do great things from a prison cell: *but . . . the things which happened unto me have fallen out rather unto the furtherance of the gospel* (Philippians 1:12 KJV). Great revolutions start in jail, and just like the apostle Paul, your prison epistle has been a rallying cry to all people—both black and white—for generations. Your letter spoke hope to us. It expressed the longings of a people for recognition, for respect, for equal access to the American Dream—for economic justice.

I too learned what it meant to be jailed unjustly—first in Mendenhall in December 1969. There was tension everywhere as our people were beginning to be mobilized to vote. Those of us who were helping with voter registration were labeled as troublemakers. I had gone to the jail to make sure a friend was not beaten. Knowing that if I went alone they would likely beat me as well, I took three carloads of children with me. We were all put in jail. As the crowd gathered outside the jail to protest, I was able to address them from my prison cell window on the second floor. I challenged them to be calm and to not fight hate with hate. We could not win with violence. We would instead boycott the merchants. We began to see that justice was an economic issue. I made up my mind while in the Mendenhall jail that this fight for justice was a worthy fight. There would be no turning back.

Our nonviolent protest and our demands for jobs for blacks, spots on the police force, and an end to police brutality were effective in drawing attention to the plight of blacks in Mississippi. And they were also effective in enraging the white power structure. Two months later twenty-three of us were arrested and put in jail in Brandon, Mississippi. I was met by the demon of racism and hatred in that place. I was tortured in the Brandon jail almost to the point of death. I was broken— almost defeated. I saw the effect of hatred in the eyes of our torturers. They were blinded by their ambition to maintain white supremacy in the South. I saw something that cannot be humanly overcome. Only the love of God could overcome such evil. I knew that if I didn't forgive, I would be overcome by the same darkness. I purposed at that moment to preach the gospel strong enough to win whites and blacks—to burn through the bigotry and hatred of racism.

Justice is birthed from the very heart of God. He revealed divine intent in the act of creation when He created man in His own image, in His own likeness. He put all people on an even plane, regardless of color—worthy of dignity and respect. And oh how our people needed to know that truth, Martin! We were not second-class citizens. God did not intend for us to grovel and beg and have a subsistence living. His heart was for each individual to work and to have their needs met through that work. So, economic justice was a fair and right claim. At its core economic justice is rooted in the proper stewardship of God's resources. The psalmist David boldly declared: *The earth is the Lord's and the fulness thereof; the world and they that dwell therein* (Ps. 24:1 KJV). Our resources have been supplied by God to be used in ways that honor Him and demonstrate our love for our fellow man.

But that's not the end of the story. The other side of that truth was that I had to wrap the image of the Southern racist in that same reality. The white racist also bore God's image and I had to allow God to love him through me. In the face of lynchings, beatings, murders, and all manner of inhumane treatment, this was not a man-sized challenge. This challenge could only be met with a power much greater than man: the love of God. In God's economy each individual was to be enriched by the other: our people were to benefit from the bounty of the white who had become enriched by free labor; the whites were to benefit from the character building truths that blacks had learned throughout and because of slavery.

All of this could have happened if America had lived up to the truth of her calling. God blessed this great nation to prosper beyond imagination. And I believe it was because of the desire of the first pilgrims to find a place where they could worship God, free from the tyranny of any government. But our nation is losing a sense of gratitude for the abundance and great bounty that God has bestowed upon us. In America we have witnessed the god of materialism sink his teeth into the fabric of the human soul. He has unleashed a spirit of rugged individualism, fueled by selfish greed. This has become normalized behavior that discourages a care for the other, and especially for the poor. The hope for America is that we will see our responsibility to care for the least among us in recognition of the truth that every person is created in the very image of God.

No, we cannot expect America to abide by the principles of love and justice of our Creator. America is not a Christian nation. But you were right, Martin, to voice strong disappointment in the church. The church should have been our strongest allies in the freedom movement and should have spoken truth to power. But instead they divorced themselves from the responsibility to bear witness to the world through the modeling of biblical love and care for one another. As you said, "they committed themselves to a completely other worldly religion which made a strange, unbiblical distinction between body and soul, between the sacred and the secular."

Sadly, that debate still rages in the church today, fifty years later. The church is still today unsure whether we are called to be fully engaged in the social needs of people. It grieves my heart to see how we have missed the opportunity to be fully engaged in the battle for economic justice. We have abundant resources yet have failed to properly steward those resources because we have accommodated an apartheid church. The church was to be the vehicle that would represent the kingdom of God in the world. We were to be a model of oneness, sharing the love of Jesus Christ one to another, and meeting the needs of one another. The church in Acts 2 is a beautiful model of this oneness: Jews and Greeks having all things in common.

Yet there is hope for the church. My greatest hope is in the new emerging church leaders who have caught the vision for true biblical oneness: multicultural churches. They operate in an almost postracial context, not seeing each other as black, white, or brown—just as brothers and sisters in Christ. This is wonderful news! I see this as a powerful move of God among His body of believers. The vision is for many others to partner together in planting similar churches. Large churches may choose to plant churches in the inner city and become intentional about their engagement together: going as a group to the inner-city church once a month, providing a percentage of their tithe to support the inner-city church.

The gospel is meant to reconcile people to God and then to each other across cultural, ethnic, and social barriers. And all of this is so the world will know we are Christians because of that oneness. That's dynamic! I want to dedicate my remaining years promoting and encouraging these types of churches.

I am seeing churches catch the vision to adopt schools and prisons and engage with them to educate and bring hope and direction to those who are suffering. We see the economics of this, but more importantly we see the hand and heart of God in this as we seek to redeem the life of each child and affirm their dignity as image bearers of our God.

When I returned to Mississippi and began the work that God called me to, there was no grand vision, Martin. I'm sure you felt the same as you went from city to city. From a boycott, to a march, to The Poor People's Campaign in Chicago, and to jail you were following the divine hand of God. Trusting His hand to lead you in ways that would bring Him honor and help our people. It was the same for us in Mendenhall, as we fell in with the people and sensed needs that demanded a response. With meager resources and no political clout, God multiplied every investment of time, heart, and energy. Little became much in His hands.

What began to emerge were three principles that would be foundational in the formation of ministry to hurting people. They are what I call the three Rs: relocation, reconciliation, and redistribution. These three components are essential in restoring dignity to the poor and needy. You embodied the first principle, relocation, when you moved to Chicago to launch the Poor People's Campaign. Living among the people allows us to live out the gospel by sharing in the suffering and pain of others. Their needs become our needs, and we have the opportunity to better the quality of their lives spiritually, physically, and emotionally as we better our own.

IT BECAME A PLACE where white and black Christians worshiped side by side. It was one of the few congregations in the South where a black pastor and white pastor shared the same pulpit.

The best picture of relocation is when Jesus took on the form of man and dwelt among us in order to give us a picture of righteousness and justice. His ultimate sacrifice of dying on the cross is the supreme example of bettering the lives of those we come to live among.

The second R, reconciliation, was based on Matthew 22:37–39 (KJV): *Jesus said unto him, Thou shalt love the Lord thy God with all thy heart, and with all thy soul, and with all thy mind. This is the first and great commandment. And the second is like unto it, Thou shalt love thy neighbor as thyself.* The heart of reconciliation is for people to be reconciled first to God and then to one another.

When we began preaching the Word in West Jackson to a few dozen people, our numbers multiplied quickly and Voice of Calvary Fellowship was formed. It became a place where white and black Christians worshiped side by side. It was one of the few congregations in the South where a black pastor and white pastor shared the same pulpit. I rejoice to see this happening more and more these days.

In an atmosphere where people have relocated to tend to the needs of others and where reconciliation has taken place, the third R, redistribution, is a natural response. It is easy to share one's wealth and resources with people you truly love and care for. There was an abundance of needs in Mendenhall and in West Jackson and God provided direction for how those needs were to be met. The People's Development, Inc. was a charity that purchased homes and sold them to the poor to help them become homeowners. Samaritan Inn was organized to provide shelter for those in distress. The first persons to stay in Samaritan Inn were white.

Nothing gave me greater joy than the opening of medical clinics so that our people could get quality health care. Prior to that time, blacks were forced to wait in segregated sections of white clinics until all of the white patients were treated. I couldn't help but think that if such a place had been available, my mother might not have died so soon.

An association of community development organizations banded together, forming the Christian Community Development Association (CCDA) and built on the three Rs of relocation, reconciliation, and redistribution. They have continued to minister to the poor in urban areas across the country. As they partner with churches to meet the enormous needs of those who are slipping through the cracks, there is reason to be encouraged.

Yes, Martin, there are rays of hope as people of faith are challenged to live out their faith in obedience to God's Word. There is hope that one day America will rise to the standard of "one nation under God", but until that happens we continue the fight for the economic and social justice that you lived for. There are many reasons why we cannot and must not be lulled to sleep by the success of a small minority. Justice denied for one is justice denied for all.

We cannot wait for economic justice because God's Word demands it. Throughout Scripture the Lord commands care for the poor. In the words of the apostle Paul, "you will be enriched in everything for all liberality, which through us is producing thanksgiving to God" (2 Corinthians 9:11 NASB). The ideal envisioned in Scripture is an equality accomplished by voluntary sharing: "For I mean not that other men be eased, and ye burdened: But by an equality, that now at this time your abundance may be a supply for their want, that their abundance also may be a supply for your want: that there may be equality: As it is written, He that had gathered much had nothing over; and he that had gathered little had no lack" (2 Corinthians 8:13–15 KJV). This is not speaking of forced redistribution. God entrusts wealth to the few so that they will share it with the many.

We cannot wait for economic justice because the creeds of America promise it. The greatest statement of justice in the history of the world is ours: "We hold these truths to be self-evident that all men are created equal and were endowed by their creator with certain inalienable rights, chief of those being the right to life, liberty, and the pursuit of happiness." No other nation in the world has such powerful principles as its foundation! And this is why I love this country so much. We have but to live out these truths so that they apply equally to every citizen of this great nation. Every moment that we delay in appropriating these principles allows the collective conscience of our nation to be dulled.

We cannot wait for economic justice because the gap between the rich and the poor is growing. I had a conversation recently with a very well-to-do gentleman. His question to me was, "Where are the poor, John?" I cringed when he asked that question, because it highlighted a sad reality. In your day, Martin, the cry was for us to "wait for a more convenient season." Nowadays the response is much like the words spoken by this gentleman. The poor are of no consequence since they are responsible for their lack. They are out of sight and out of mind—many locked away in prisons, others languishing in a substandard existence.

All the while the rich are getting richer. I won't bore you with statistics, but they are alarming. And they bear out the fact that the bottom layer of the pyramid is getting wider and wider as more Americans struggle to survive. I have no doubt, Martin, that if you were here today, these are the people that you would be championing and fighting for.

We cannot wait for economic justice because minds are wasting. I was so proud of you, Martin. You were brilliant, educated, and eloquent—you represented us so well. You were a picture of how an educated black man could speak the truth to power and be heard. I dropped out of school between the third and fifth grade. So I got my education as I lived. The hand of the Almighty God on my life kept me from suffering the fate of so many others who were just like me—the uneducated poor.

In your day, Martin, you saw the marches and boycotts as a way for the Negro to release his pent-up resentments and latent frustrations. If his repressed emotions were not released in nonviolent ways, they would seek expression through violence. I regret most of all that this is happening in our urban centers across this nation today.

What is most needed is not a handout but quality education that leads to quality employment and economic stability. A friend of mine once told me that the best welfare system is a good job. He was right. The access to good jobs is limited to those who qualify by virtue of their education or their connections to those in positions of influence. The United Negro College Fund's slogan is "a mind is a terrible thing to waste." This is a powerful truth. Quality education opens the door for the poor to achieve and to secure their part of the American dream.

And finally, *we cannot wait for economic justice because time is running out.* It's been fifty years, Martin, since your letter was written. That's a good deal of time to have made many more significant advances in the cause that you gave your life for. And there is a time of accounting coming. The One who is the ultimate owner of everything—the Creator God—has entrusted the management of His world to us as stewards. We've been charged to subdue the earth, develop its potential, and to provide for one another out of its bounty. And just like the master in Matthew 25, He is coming back to settle the accounts. When He returns His standards may make some of us uncomfortable: *But when the Son of Man comes in His glory, and all the angels with Him, then He will sit on His glorious throne. All the nations will be gathered before Him; and He will separate them from one another, as the shepherd separates the sheep from the goats; and He will put the sheep on His right, and the goats on the left. Then the King will say to those on His right, "Come, you who are blessed of My Father, inherit the kingdom prepared for you from the foundation of the world. For I was hungry, and you gave Me something to eat; I was thirsty, and you gave Me something to drink; I was a stranger, and you invited Me in; naked, and you clothed Me; I was sick, and you visited Me; I was in prison, and you came to Me"* (Matthew 25:31–36 NASB).

So time is running out for those who have opportunity to do justice. But it's also running out for those who are in desperate need.

There are generations of people who have lived and died in poverty in this nation. That should not be. Not in the richest nation of the world. I pray that we will do good while it is yet day.

And yes, Martin, please forgive my being so personal on this last point. Time is running out for me. God has been good to me. I've lived a good life. The psalmist perhaps said it best in Psalm 90 (KJV): *Lord, thou hast been our dwelling place in all generations . . . For all our days are passed away in thy wrath; we spend our years as a tale that is told. The days of our years are threescore years and ten; and if by reason of strength they be fourscore years, yet is their strength labour and sorrow . . . So, teach us to number our days, that we might apply our hearts unto wisdom.*

I'm eighty-three years old now. I can begin to see the setting of the sun and there is a sense of urgency to pass along to coming generations the principles and teachings that have kept me all these years. If I had to boil it down to the simplest of truths, it would be this one thing: Jesus—Jesus alone. He is the pearl of great price. *Without Him* nothing else matters; *with* Him you need nothing else.

All my life I had a longing, For a drink from some clear spring,
That I hoped would quench the burning, Of the thirst I felt within.
Feeding on the husks around me, Till my strength was almost gone,
Longed my soul for something better, Only still to hunger on.
Poor I was and sought for riches, Something that would satisfy,
But the dust I gathered round me, Only mocked my soul's sad cry.
Well of water ever springing, Bread of life so rich and free,
Untold wealth that never faileth, My Redeemer is to me.
Hallelujah! I have found Him
Whom my soul so long has craved!
Jesus satisfies my longings,
Through His blood I now am saved.[1]

Martin, I'm satisfied with my Savior and with His leading. I'm satisfied that a life spent serving Him is a life worth living. And, yes, I'm satisfied that serving our fellow man with the glorious gospel is the only thing that really matters in life. I'm satisfied . . . and I'll see you in the morning, my friend.

Dear Dr. King,

You were right. You prophesied, "If today's church does not recapture the sacrificial spirit of the early church, it will . . . be dismissed as an irrelevant social club with no meaning for the 20th century."

But we have lost more than a sacrificial spirit. One of your prophetic heirs, Carl Ellis, has made clear that many black and white churches have become "irrelevant social clubs" because they have lost the God-centered, Christ-exalting, Bible-saturated gospel. God has been sold for good agendas.

There are times I wished you had made the biblical gospel clearer. But I am sure you would agree that the power you wielded was rooted in God. Today, as I look at the gospel-weak white and black churches, I would say that both need a transcendent reference point in the sovereignty, supremacy, and centrality of God, expressed supremely in the gospel of Jesus Christ

God-centered, Christ-exalting, Bible-saturated churches where the gospel is cherished—these are the birthplace of the kind of racial harmony that gives long-term glory to God and long-term gospel good to the world.

Again you were right about the folly of passive waiting. Biblical waiting is not passive. It does not compromise. Nothing that needs changing changes without effort.

Some may have quoted, "Wait for the Lord; be strong, and let your heart take courage; wait for the Lord!" (Psalm 27:14). But this call to wait for the Lord never meant stop doing what He commanded us to do in the pursuit of holy goals. Waiting for the Lord means our action is essential, but His is decisive. The farmer must wait for the harvest. But no one works harder than the farmer.

Thank you for your sacrifices. May our Lord Jesus hasten the day when the terms "white church" and "black church" will be unintelligible.

John Piper

2

WAITING FOR AND HASTENING THE DAY OF MULTIETHNIC BEAUTY

John Piper

A PERSONAL AND CULTURAL ISLAND

I was seventeen years old when Martin Luther King wrote *Letter from a Birmingham Jail*. Stephen Oates called it, "the most eloquent and learned expression of the goals and philosophy of the nonviolent movement ever written."[1] But I was too consumed with my own petty insecurities to take note. Pimples, nervousness, girls (wondering what they thought). I was like an island of self-concern in a sea of social turmoil.

If I were the only one, this would be a trivial detail. But alas, the world—especially the white American world of the 1950s and '60s—had drifted from a World War passion against the horrors of German Nazism and Japanese expansionism to an insulated stupor of suburban security. Basement bomb shelters were the symbol of social engagement.

When Paul Simon (of Simon and Garfunkel) wrote his song "I Am a Rock" in 1965, it was not a celebration. It was an indictment. It indicted those who would isolate themselves from others, who would not deal with the important yet uncomfortable issues of life. To avoid conflict, the person would "touch no one and no one touches me. I am a rock, I am an island."[3]

Not only was I an island of immature, individual insecurities; I was

57

part of a cultural island. I lived in a white suburb of Greenville, South Carolina, across the highway from a Christian university where interracial dating was forbidden until 2000. That highway, and my all-white public high school were named after the confederate lieutenant general Wade Hampton. The school colors were red and grey, and they were named the Rebels.

I attended an all-white Baptist church on Wade Hampton Boulevard, which passed a resolution in the early sixties that blacks would not be allowed to attend—a rule that my mother defied at my sister's wedding in December 1962, when she welcomed a black family to sit with all the guests. They were Lucy's family. Lucy was our "help." She came on Tuesdays and Saturdays and helped my mother clean. But I didn't really know Lucy. She was from another island.

I found out later during college (when it had started to matter) that a shirttail relative, who also attended the church, was a member of the KKK. He seemed quite proud of it. It just came out one afternoon at a pizza party when I was home on vacation, and was passed over with, perhaps, the awkwardness of a *faux pas*. Risky, moral courage was not the dominant trait of my island.

A HIGH PRICE FOR FREEDOM, AND A SLOW BEGINNING

Just a hundred years earlier, the population of South Carolina was about 700,000. Sixty percent were African Americans (420,000), and all but 9,000 of these were slaves. On December 20, 1860, South Carolina was the first state to secede from the Union. Three weeks later, the Civil War began in Charleston, South Carolina.

Newer estimates of the casualties of the conflict are now around 750,000 soldiers who died in the Civil War.[3] That would be equivalent, in proportion to America's population, to about 7.5 million Americans today. It was a high price.

The victory of full acceptance for African Americans into all the corners of American life is still in the making. It was a slow and painful beginning. Two years after the Civil War in 1867, 535 African Americans were lynched.[4] A dozen years after the Civil War, the efforts of reconstruction were spent, and the solidification of segregation and disenfranchisement was underway.

There were flashes of hope followed by enduring darkness. By 1890, the former Confederate states had written new constitutions that put in place the same two-tiered system of justice that had existed in the slave era. Jim Crow was established[5] and things often went backwards For example, in 1897 Louisiana had 137,000 registered black voters. Three years later, that number had been reduced to 5,000.[6]

NINETY YEARS OF FREEDOM
FOR SEPARATE DRINKING FOUNTAINS

Fast-forward ninety years from April 9, 1865 to 1955, when I was a nine-year-old in Greenville. I was learning the rules of the island. Enforced segregation was pervasive. For some reason an image from the Kress five-and-dime store is blazoned on my memory: two water fountains eighteen inches apart from each other on the wall. The sign over one said, "White." The sign over the other said, "Colored." To this day my stomach turns at what that communicated to whites and blacks. Before there was AIDS to be afraid of, there was blackness. You might get some of it on you.

> **I NEVER SAW ONE equal provision for blacks.**
> **And not only was it not equal, it was not respectful,**
> **it was not just, and it was not loving; therefore,**
> **it was not Christian.**

The shame and ugliness of it was everywhere you turned. Not only drinking fountains but also public restrooms, public schools, public swimming pools, bus seating, housing, restaurants, hospital waiting rooms, dentist waiting rooms, bus station waiting rooms, and—with their own kind of enforcement—churches. In spite of all the rationalizations, it was not "separate but equal." I never saw one equal provision for blacks. And not only was it not equal, it was not respectful, it was not just, and it was not loving; therefore, it was not Christian. It was ugly and demeaning. It was a way of keeping the waves of reform from breaking over the peace and comfort of our island.

NEAR AND YET SO FAR

Three and a half miles across town from where I grew up, in the same city, five years older than I, another little boy was growing up on the other island. His name was Jesse Jackson. Jackson was born October 8, 1941, at his home on 20 Haynie Street in Greenville. When he was thirteen, the family moved to a newly constructed housing project, Fieldcrest Village (now Jesse Jackson Townhomes)—three miles to the east. His biographer describes the neighborhood:

> . . . a dingy warren of flimsy little houses, with plank porch railings ranked with rusted coffee cans that, in the summer, held rufflings of geraniums and caladiums. Each house was perched on a tiny, grassless, rutted yard some scattered with wood chips and upturned washtubs and old tires and bluish puddles of pitched-out dishwater, others whisked clean with straw brooms and enclosed by spindly fences assembled out of scraps of boards and wire, with walkways bordered by bits of brick and cement block and broken bottles set in neat parallel lines in the dirt.[7]

Our worlds—our islands—were so close and yet so far apart. His mother, Helen, loved the same Christian radio station my mother did—WMUU, the voice of Bob Jones University. The radio waves reached across the unnavigable waters that divided us. But I never made the slightest effort to sail those few miles.

WHAT LUCY TAUGHT ME

I didn't know a single black person—except Lucy. And my relationship with Lucy taught me, in a surprising way, that it is possible to like someone, and even feel deep affection for someone and treat her graciously, while considering her inferior and as someone to be kept at a distance. This in turn has taught me that those who defend the noble spirit of some Southern slaveholders by pointing to how nice they were to their slaves seem to be naïve about what makes a relationship degrading. I also cried when my dog got run over.

But this chapter is not the story of John Piper's racism and redemption. I told that story in *Bloodlines*.[8] This chapter is the story of how to wait for God and hasten the day of multiethnic beauty. I will try to make plain what that means.

AN ALTERNATIVE TO BLOODSHED

As we came to the middle of the twentieth century, the flashpoint of racial justice—the fair treatment of people on the basis of character and action, not on the basis of the color of their skin or their ethnic origins—had arrived. It had been long in coming. The first black slaves had been brought to America in 1565 as part of the colonization of St. Augustine, Florida. So, when Martin Luther King came on the scene, black-white relations, based on perceived racial inferiority and rooted in man-stealing and slavery, had been part of American life for four hundred years. The Civil War had removed slavery, but not oppression.

By the 1960s that centuries-long oppression had produced two forces in the African American communities: one complacent, the other seething on the brink of violence. Martin Luther King saw himself as a middle way, not an extremist. He believed if it were not for the nonviolent protests he was leading, the streets of America would soon be "flowing with blood" in a "frightening racial nightmare." I think he was probably right about that.

IN BIRMINGHAM TO PREVENT "BOMBINGHAM"

That's why he was in Birmingham in the spring of 1963. On April 3, Martin Luther King issued the "Birmingham Manifesto" (not the *Letter*). He was thirty-four years old, married, and with four children, one of them only five days old. The manifesto called for all lunch counters, restrooms, and drinking fountains in downtown department stores to be desegregated.

Some called the city the most segregated city in the country. Its bombings and torchings of black churches and homes had given it the name "Bombingham"—the "Johannesburg of the South." That day sixty-five blacks staged sit-ins in five stores, and Police Commissioner Eugene "Bull" Connor dragged twenty of them away to jail.

King arrived with unparalleled eloquence in the service of nonviolence. In nightly meetings in the black churches, he rallied the troops:

> We did not hesitate to call our movements an army. But it was a special army, with no supplies but its sincerity. No uniform but its determination, no arsenal, except its faith, no currency but its conscience. It was an army that would move but not maul. It was an army that would sing but not slay. It was an army to storm bastions of hatred, to lay siege to the fortress of segregation, to surround symbols of discrimination.[9]

THE WHITE "CALL FOR UNITY"

On April 13, Good Friday, King and his team refused to follow a court injunction that forbade peaceful marching. Such injunctions had been used to tie up peaceful direct action for years. Not this time. King met the barricades and the shouting Bull Conner. He knelt beside his friend Ralph Abernathy, and was thrown into the paddy wagon and taken to the Birmingham city jail. This was the thirteenth time King had been arrested.

He was put in solitary confinement without mattress, pillow, or blanket. His situation improved when Attorney General Robert Kennedy asked why he was in solitary confinement. On Tuesday, April 16, he was brought a newspaper in prison, the *Birmingham News*, where eight white clergymen had published their "Call for Unity."

We are now confronted by a series of demonstrations by some of our Negro citizens, directed and led in part by outsiders [a reference to King]. We recognize the natural impatience of people who feel that their hopes are slow in being realized. But we are convinced that these demonstrations are unwise and untimely....

We do not believe that these days of new hope are days when extreme measures are justified in Birmingham.... We further strongly urge our own Negro community to withdraw support from these demonstrations, and to unite locally in working peacefully for a better Birmingham. When rights are consistently denied, a cause should be pressed in the courts and in negotiations among local leaders, and not in the streets. We appeal to both our white and Negro citizenry to observe the principles of law and order and common sense.[10]

UNLEASHED ELOQUENCE
FROM BIRMINGHAM JAIL

This was the spark that ignited King's eloquence in his "Letter from a Birmingham Jail." To their admonition that Negroes overcome their "natural impatience" and renounce "extreme measures," King responded:

> For years now I have heard the word "Wait!" It rings in the ear of every Negro with piercing familiarity. This "Wait" has almost always meant "Never." We must come to see, with one of our distinguished jurists, that "justice too long delayed is justice denied."[11]

Then King rises to his most vivid and compelling picture of why the call to wait rings so hollow:

> We have waited for more than 340 years for our constitutional and God-given rights . . . but we still creep at horse-and-buggy pace toward gaining a cup of coffee at a lunch counter.

> Perhaps it is easy for those who have never felt the stinging darts of segregation to say, "Wait." But when you have seen vicious mobs lynch your mothers and fathers at will and drown your sisters and brothers at whim; when you have seen hate-filled policeman curse, kick, and even kill your black brothers and sisters; when you see the vast majority of your 20 million Negro brothers smothering in an airtight cage of poverty in the midst of an affluent society; when you suddenly find your tongue twisted and your speech stammering as you seek to explain to your six-year-old daughter why she cannot go to the public amusement park that has just been advertised on television, and see tears welling up in her eyes when she's told that Funtown is closed to colored children, and see ominous

clouds of inferiority beginning to form in her little mental sky, and see her beginning to distort her personality by developing an unconscious bitterness toward white people; when you have to concoct an answer for a five-year-old son who is asking, "Daddy, why do white people treat colored people so mean?"; when you take a cross-country drive and find it necessary to sleep night after night in the uncomfortable corners of your automobile because no motel will accept you; when you are humiliated day in and day out by nagging signs reading "white" and "colored"; when your first name becomes "Nigger," your middle name becomes "Boy" (however old you are), and your last name becomes "John," and your wife and mother are never given the respected title "Mrs."; when you are harried by day and haunted by night by the fact that you are a Negro, living constantly at tiptoe stance, never quite knowing what to expect next, and are plagued with inner fears and outer resentments; when you are forever fighting a degenerating sense of "nobodiness"—then you will understand why we find it difficult to wait. There comes a time when the cup of endurance runs over, and men are no longer willing to be plunged into the abyss of despair. I hope, sirs, you can understand our legitimate and unavoidable impatience.[12]

"NO LONGER"

When I first read these words many years ago, they stunned me. I had never read anything about racial relations or the civil rights movement more moving than these words. Every word rang true. And the cumulative force was devastating. One can sense the wonder that, in the providence of God, such a voice had been heard above the cries of those days.

King was not done explaining. He used his method because he truly believed that waiting would be forever without it.

You may well ask: "Why direct action? Why sit-ins, marches and so forth? Isn't negotiation a better path?" You are quite right in calling for negotiation. Indeed, this is the very purpose of direct action. Nonviolent direct action seeks to create such a crisis and foster such a tension that a community which has constantly refused to negotiate is forced to confront the issue. It seeks to so dramatize the issue that it can no longer be ignored.[13]

How long would the wrong be ignored? King's answer: "No longer." It was a flashpoint in our nation. A midcentury wind. The islands were colliding. Bob Dylan released his song, "Blowin' in the Wind" the same year King published "Letter from a Birmingham Jail." They both asked the same question: How long? "How many years . . . How many times" before things would change, Dylan asked.

Yes, it was an antiwar song. But in the middle of the song were the words that in the 1960s could not be heard without racial implications: "Yes, how many years can some people exist/Before they're allowed to be free?"[14]

AWAKENING

When Peter, Paul, and Mary sang "Blowin' in the Wind" in March 1963, it bumped "Puppy Love" from the top of the charts. What this symbolized was that a lot of young John Pipers were about to be shaken loose from their immature, insulated, petty insecurities and catapulted into a bigger world. The personal islands of isolation and ignorance and indifference, and the cultural islands of segregation and suspicion and derision were all sinking in the sea. For me it was the sea of gospel awakening. A Jesus awakening.

JESUS, LOVE, CHURCH

For all of King's theological and personal flaws, he pointed us in the right direction: to Jesus rather than self, to love rather than hate, and to the sacrificial church rather than the religious social club. His "Letter" asked us:

> Was not Jesus an extremist for love: "Love your enemies, bless them that curse you, do good to them that hate you, and pray for them which despitefully use you, and persecute you"? Was not Amos an extremist for justice: "Let justice roll to down like waters and righteousness like an ever-flowing stream"? Was not Paul an extremist for the Christian gospel: "I bear in my body the marks of the Lord Jesus"? Was not Martin Luther an extremist: "Here I stand; I cannot do otherwise, so help me God"? And John Bunyan: "I will stay in jail to the end of my days before I make a butchery of my conscience." And Abraham Lincoln: "Thus this nation cannot survive half slave and half free." And Thomas Jefferson: "We hold these truths to be self-evident, that all men are created equal . . ." So the question is not whether we will be extremist, but what kind of extremist we will be. Will we be extremists for hate or for love? . . .

MAINLINE PROTESTANT denominations, white and black, in large measure, have sold their gospel soul for the pottage of trendy social issues mingled with secular unbelief.

There was a time when the church was very powerful—in the time when the early Christians rejoiced at being deemed worthy to suffer for what they believed. In those days the church was not merely a thermometer that recorded the ideas and principles of popular opinion; it was a thermostat that transformed the mores of society.... But the judgment of God is upon the church [today] as never before. If today's church does not recapture the sacrificial spirit of the early church, it will lose its authenticity, forfeit the loyalty of millions, and be dismissed as an irrelevant social club with no meaning for the 20th century.[15]

A JUDGMENT ON BOTH YOUR HOUSES

In the last fifty years this judgment has come upon white and black churches alike. Mainline Protestant denominations, white and black, in large measure, have sold their gospel soul for the pottage of trendy social issues mingled with secular unbelief. And many trendy, so-called evangelical churches marched right behind them.

But this has not turned out quite the way Martin Luther King envisaged it. The seeds of gospel displacement were already present in his message. Few people have analyzed these developments since King's day more profoundly than Carl Ellis in his book, *Free at Last*. Nothing I have read eclipses the insights of this book in understanding what has happened in black and white churches since the civil rights movement, and how they relate to each other.

THE MISSING GOD

What Ellis sees so clearly is that the so-called white and black churches have both been compromised theologically. Ellis's vision for the rebuilding of a God-centered black culture is profoundly relevant for the rebuilding of a God-centered white American evangelicalism. One sentence took hold of me in 2001 when I first read this book. Ellis wrote, "White historians had sold us a bill of goods by leaving Black folks out; Black secularists sold us a bill of goods by leaving God out."[16]

The reason that sentence cuts deeply both ways is not mainly because it criticizes white historians as bad historians, or black secularists as bad theologians, but mainly because it makes us focus on that particular weakness of the black community that it had taken straight from the dominant white culture, namely, secular humanism, in contradiction to the deeper, more authentic, God-soaked roots of the historic black culture in America—and, I would add, also in contradiction to the deeper, more authentic, God-soaked roots of the white evangelical culture in America.

THE PROBLEM DEEPER THAN ETHNOCENTRISM

There is no doubt in my mind that God raised up Martin Luther King in the middle of the twentieth century to accomplish the gracious biblical purposes of truth and justice. But it is also true that King was already influenced by the theologically liberal white establishment at Crozer Theological Seminary and Boston University. The great God-centeredness of the gospel of Jesus Christ's death and resurrection to propitiate the wrath of God and save sinners from hell and from sins like racism—this gospel had already slipped to the margins of King's message.

What Ellis makes clear is that something deeper than ethnocentrism has been at work in the fifty years since Martin Luther King's vision was heralded so powerfully. Ellis's ax cuts through to the compromises of white and black churches alike that have lamed us deeply. These compromises certainly include the kinds of ethnocentrism that infect our lives and push us apart. But there is something deeper. His aim is the rebuilding of a God-centered Christianity, not "Christianityism."[17] He calls for authentic, God-centered, Christ-exalting, Bible-saturated Christianity out of white and black and every other color. You feel Ellis's two-edged sword in sentences like these:

Black is truly beautiful, but it is not beautiful as a god. As a god it is too small. Afrocentrism is truly magnificent, but it is not magnificent as an absolute. As an absolute, it will infect us with the kind of bigotry we've struggled against in others for centuries. . . . Whenever we seek to understand our situation without [the] transcendent reference point [of the Word of God] we fail to find the answer to our crisis. The white man's religion has failed us [namely, Christianity-ism]. The Arab ethnic religion has failed us and will fail us again.[18]

White systems that adapt the gospel's radical message to the spirit of the age have failed. Efforts at establishing churches and movements on "black is beautiful" have failed. We need a bigger vision, a deeper vision. We need a transcendent reference point! We need the supremacy of God! The centrality of God! The Word of God! The radical gospel of Jesus Christ in its fullest and deepest biblical proportions.

When I first read Ellis's book in July 2001, everything in me was crying, "Amen," not about the weaknesses of the *black* church but about the so-called *white* church—my own puny-god, market-driven, materialistic, middle-class, comfort-seeking, truth-compromising, wishy-washy, white, evangelical, American church. What became clearer to me then than ever was that what both communities need is a transcendent reference point in the sovereignty of God and the supremacy of God and the centrality of God in all things, expressed supremely in the gospel of Jesus Christ.

FIRST THE BRIDE, THEN THE WORLD

One of the implications of this radical, God-centered, Christ-exalting, Bible-saturated, gospel-cherishing passion is that the pursuit of increasingly natural and beautiful racial diversity and justice and harmony will happen first in the churches where these values are loved. I don't mean that these churches will be blind or indifferent to the wider secular culture. Rather I mean that the community where God is central, and Christ is exalted, and the Bible is believed, and the gospel is cherished—this is where God-centered, Christ-exalting, Bible-saturated, gospel-cherishing racial diversity and harmony can be advanced. And from these churches, only God knows how deep and vast the wider cultural transformation might be.

If the church focuses on efforts toward racial diversity and justice and harmony where God is *not* central, and Christ is not exalted, and the Bible is not believed, and the gospel is not cherished, the inevitable result will be what we have seen for the last fifty years—the marginalization of God, the centralization of noble slogans, and the loss of power to change human hearts and the institutions they create. Where the fruit of the gospel is made the gospel, the power of the gospel to produce its fruit dies.

IT DOES NOT COME BY PASSIVE WAITING

This primary goal—the goal to lead churches, not first the entire secular culture, into the beauty of ethnic and racial diversity and justice and harmony that Christ purchased by His blood (Revelation 5:9)— this primary goal is urgent. It will not arrive by waiting for it passively. Martin Luther King was right that traditions that are blind to the need for change do not change without effort. Mere waiting does not work. There must be pursuit.[19]

But someone may ask, doesn't the Bible say, "Wait for the LORD; be strong, and let your heart take courage; wait for the LORD!" (Psalm 27:14)? Yes it does. But this call to wait for the Lord never meant stop doing what God commanded you to do in the pursuit of holy goals.

Recall, for example, that when Israel murmured against Moses that they were trapped by Pharaoh at the Red Sea, he said, *Fear not, stand firm, and see the salvation of the LORD, which he will work for you today.*

. . . *The* LORD *will fight for you, and you have only to be silent* (Exodus 14:13–14). That sounds like the right thing to do was wait and nothing else. But God comes and says to Moses, *Why do you cry to me? Tell the people of Israel to go forward. Lift up your staff, and stretch out your hand over the sea and divide it, that the people of Israel may go through the sea on dry ground* (Exodus 14:15–16).

God was not telling the people to stop waiting for Him. He was showing them *how* to wait for Him. God was going to work a miracle for them. He was going to divide the sea. That would be a miracle. They could not make that happen. They could only look for it. But God was going to use Moses to do it. And He was going to do it for a people on the march.

WAITING FOR AND HASTENING THE DAY

This is how it always is. Waiting for the Lord means acting with the confidence and expectation that the only way your action will bear fruit is that God will show up. *I worked harder than any of them, though it was not I, but the grace of God that is with me* (1 Corinthians 15:10). Paul waited for the grace of God *as* he worked. Or again he said, *I will not venture to speak of anything except what Christ has accomplished through me to bring the Gentiles to obedience—by word and deed* (Romans 15:18). Paul spoke, Paul acted, but God brought about the obedience of the Gentiles. Or again, *I planted, Apollos watered, but God gave the growth* (1 Corinthians 3:6). James wrote farmers must be patient and wait for the harvest (James 5:7). But in the meantime, no one works harder than the farmer.

So yes, we must wait for God. Only God can accomplish the glorious miracle of God-centered, Christ-exalting, Bible-saturated, gospel-cherishing ethnic and racial diversity, justice, and harmony in our churches. But this waiting on God's miraculous in-breaking is intensely active. As with the day of God, so with the day of racial glory: *What sort of people ought you to be in lives of holiness and godliness, waiting for* and hastening *the coming of the day of God* (2 Peter 3:11–12). There is a holiness that hastens.

Lord, teach us how to wait for You in such a faith-filled, Spirit-dependent, radically active way that we hasten the day when the terms "white church" and "black church" will be unintelligible.

Dear Dr. King,

It's been over fifty years since you declared that we can wait no longer for biblical justice. I am writing because I have to say "thank you." If God had not used you and the other courageous men and women of the civil rights movement to pave the way, the doors that have been opened to me and the opportunities afforded me would have never happened.

As a teenager I fell in love with the Word of God. The more I read it, the more I was captured by His description of the church—what it should be and represent in the world. Ephesians 2 was like a powerful magnet pulling me back time and again to the compelling description and vision of God's church, a reconciled community. As that vision wrapped itself around my imagination and heart, your emphasis on love and integration fueled that vision within me.

By the time I was sixteen, there were two things I knew I wanted to do the rest of my life. Preach the Word of God and serve in a context in which the unity of the body of Christ was being demonstrated. The second thing has proven to be the most costly and painful and yet the most rewarding and joyful.

So many times on the journey, I almost caved in and walked away; but God wouldn't let me. He gave me encouragement through like-minded brothers, who'd also been influenced by you.

Today I serve as the first African American pastor of a predominantly white church growing toward ethnic diversity and that vision God emblazoned on my heart years ago.

To men like you, I owe a profound debt of gratitude for staying the course.

Thank you. You are helping me finish mine.

Pastor Crawford Loritts

3

A PAINFUL JOYFUL JOURNEY

Crawford W. Loritts Jr.

A FEW YEARS AGO our oldest son, Bryan, and I were speaking at the Cove, the Billy Graham conference center in Asheville, North Carolina. Less than an hour's drive down Interstate 40 is where four generations of Loritts were born and raised. We hadn't been there in years so Bryan and I decided to visit the old homestead.

As we crossed the railroad tracks and spotted the small church that stood on the land once owned by my grandfather, my mind was flooded with memories and stories my dad and uncles talked about and shared with me. Behind the church is a cemetery where several generations of Loritts are buried, including my grandparents (Milton and Anna) and my great-grandfather Peter, the former slave. As we looked at the grave markers, I had the joy and privilege of sharing with Bryan who these people were and what they lived for.

On our way back to Asheville, we stopped for lunch. There in the restaurant as we continued talking about their lives and the challenges of their moment in history, I was ambushed by emotion and I began to weep. I said to Bryan, "Son, those folks paid our tuition." They paid for what they were denied and to a large degree we enjoy what we didn't pay for. We dare not forget their tears, suffering, prayers, and hopes for something better for their children and grandchildren. Their dreams had to be pushed forward to a time that they could not experience. But their hope was that just maybe their children and their children's children would enjoy the harvest that was sown in suffering and fertilized by tears. That's what they and millions of other African Americans paid for.

Both Bryan and I were revisited by a fresh sense of humility because of the stewardship that has been placed in our hands. What has been given to us is very expensive. Lives have been given for the freedom and access we enjoy.

The civil rights movement, championed by Martin Luther King Jr., declared that we were no longer willing to be marginalized and thrust aside as necessary but nonessential "components" of the American fabric. Every human being has been created in the image of God and has dignity written on their soul. It was time that we were treated in light of the value and dignity given to us by our Creator.

Nowhere is this perspective more clearly given than in a letter King wrote on April 16, 1963. He was in jail in Birmingham, Alabama, for protesting the flagrant racial injustice of that city. The letter has come to be known simply as the "Letter from a Birmingham Jail." I am sobered by a particular line in that letter: "We will have to repent in this generation not merely for the hateful words and actions of the bad people but the appalling silence of the good people." It was time for holy impatience.

Now, more than fifty years later, I am writing this letter back to that Birmingham jail to say thank you and to give a progress report through the lens of my journey.

I am a child of the great migration. Between the early 1900s until about 1970, millions of African Americans left the South and flooded cities like New York, Newark, Philadelphia, Detroit, Chicago, and Los Angeles. They were tired of the oppressive segregation (Jim Crow) and they were looking for jobs that provided more opportunity for their families. In 1942 Crawford and Sylvia Loritts (my parents) moved from North Carolina to Newark, New Jersey. I have two older sisters. We were born in Newark.

For the first twelve years of my life we lived in what was then called the central ward. Little did I know that the environment in which I grew up would serve as the context in which I would minister for now more than forty years. Serving in diverse, multiethnic contexts is not abnormal to me. It was how I grew up.

The central ward of the 1950s and early 60s was a diverse, working-class community. On the first floor of our apartment building lived the Phillibaccus family. They were Greek and we all did birthday parties together. I went to school with and played with John Sangiovanni, Rocco Bonaviture, Lloyd Cotton, and Freddie Gains, to name a few. We did more than hang out together; we were in each other's homes. One of my dad's best friends was a man named O'Sullivan. I don't remember his first name. We called him Uncle Sully. He was Irish. Growing up during those formative years, I never thought I had to make a choice as to who my friends should be.

Virtually everything I did was integrated except for church. We attended Trinity AME and this was a powerful influence shaping my young life. My parents made sure we knew where we came from. We were told stories of our parents and great-grandparents. My dad made sure we knew about Peter Loritts, the former slave. They wanted us to grow up with an appreciation for the price that was paid for our access and opportunity. Mom and Pop wanted us to honor and respect those who went before us. This was a pretty big deal to them. My parents were not perfect, but I am profoundly grateful to God that my mother and father gave me the gifts of security and identity. I did not grow up feeling uncomfortable around white people; nor did I feel the need for their approval in order for me to feel good about myself. This sense of security, however, would be threatened and tested in the years ahead.

As I look back now, I can appreciate the sense of sacrifice and "future" that so many in my parents' generation had. Racism meant denied and limited opportunities for them. That's the reason why Pop would really get after me and my sisters when we weren't doing our best or what he thought we were capable of. He would then give us the speech: "Do you know why I am working so hard? It's because I want you to have better and do better than I could do." His point was obvious. We had more opportunity than his generation ever did, so don't blow it.

> **I KNEW INSTINCTIVELY** that this sign wasn't about a dedicated entrance for special people. No, whoever put that sign up didn't think that we were worth walking through the front door.

My first encounter with segregation came when I was six or seven years old. More than half a century later, I remember it as if it happened this morning. We were travelling from New Jersey to North Carolina to visit some relatives. Evidently Pop had been driving most of the night and in the wee hours of the morning—somewhere in southern Virginia—he pulled into a service station to get some gas, stretch his legs, and get some coffee. Pop had his hand on my shoulder as we walked toward this 1950s version of a convenience store. As we approached the door, I saw the sign. I could read. There it was, as big as day: "Colored Served in Rear." I knew I was "colored." I may have been only six or seven, but I knew instinctively that this sign wasn't about a dedicated entrance for special people. No, whoever put that sign up didn't think that we were worth walking through the front door. I said to my father, "Pop, why do we have to go around the back?" He leaned down and said, "Son, close your mouth and follow me." And I did. We went to the bathroom. Pop got his coffee. We were on our way.

It was the first time I had experienced overt racism. But I was grateful for Uncle Sully and for the Phillabaccus family. They loved us and they wouldn't treat us this way.

In 1962 we moved to Plainfield, New Jersey. That's where I went to junior high and high school. It is also where at age thirteen I became a follower of Christ. I grew up in a Christian home but for some reason the gospel didn't "stick" until that second Sunday in January 1964. I fell in love with Jesus and I developed a growing desire to not only read and study the Bible but to share Christ and God's Word with others.

But this was also a time in which the civil rights movement was gaining increased visibility and momentum. It was a force to be reckoned with. There was no turning back. Nightly we witnessed on television church bombings, dogs biting demonstrators, blasts from fire hoses pinning people to the ground, police using billy clubs on marchers, freedom riders killed, and civil rights leaders assassinated. The cameras "spoke" eloquently and revealingly. The nation could no longer ignore, deny, or placate millions of African Americans who wanted to be treated with dignity and justice.

I was an African American teenager trying to put all of this together and figure it out. I was captured by King's message of love and his refusal to respond with hate and violence. I was struck by the prayer meetings held by many who were a part of the movement, asking God for freedom and substantive change in race relations in this country.

So many things were swirling around in my head and in my soul during this time as I tried to figure out my place in all of this. This growing tidal wave did not feel distant to me. It felt very personal. As I watched protestors ridiculed, beaten, and herded off to jail, in my mind's eye I saw my cousins, aunts, and uncles. I remembered the family reunions and the stories my parents and relatives shared about what they faced and how they overcame. I imagined what Peter Loritts, the patriarch and former slave, endured and suffered. And burned in my mind was that sign: "Colored Served in Rear."

As a follower of Christ, the seeds of how God would use me and the calling He would give me were being sown and germinated during this time. Let me explain. As far back as I can remember, I've always had very close friends who were not African Americans. This was the case during my high school years. I never felt the need to pull back from them because of how black people were being treated. They were my friends. Our school was integrated and I had both white and black friends; I never felt as if I had to choose my black friends over my white friends in order to prove my ethnic loyalty. This was not some courageous, heroic stand. It was how I was raised. And I knew that my dad would say that I would be less than a man if I allowed someone or some group to tell me who I could or couldn't associate with.

But there was something deeper, richer, and more compelling forming in my heart. This would be the anchor that would hold me and the truth that would shape my life and the trajectory of my ministry for years to come.

During these teenage years, I fell in love with the Word of God. The more I read it, the more I was captured by God's description of the church and what it should be and represent in the world. I was drawn to Jesus' prayer in John 17 where He pleaded with His Father that we, His followers, would be unified. Ephesians chapter 2 was like a powerful magnet pulling me back time and again to the apostle Paul's compelling description and vision of God's church, a reconciled community. I felt a growing conviction in my heart that unity and reconciliation were not some mystical concepts but should be a reality. What if God really meant us to visibly demonstrate the unity of His church? What would it look like? Would I be willing to do this?

Again, this calling, this vision, began to wrap itself around my imagination and my heart. Interestingly enough, Dr. King's emphasis on love and integration fueled this vision in me. By the time I was sixteen, there were two things that I knew I wanted to spend the rest of my life doing: 1) Preaching the Word of God, and 2) serving in a context in which the unity of the body of Christ would be demonstrated.

It is that second thing that has proven to be the most costly and painful and at the same time the most rewarding. At this stage in my life, it is a great source of joy.

In the fall of 1968 I began my freshman year at Philadelphia College of the Bible (now Cairn University). I cannot say enough about the powerful influence this school and my four years there had on my life and ministry (that's at least another essay). The foundation for how I teach and preach the Word of God to this very day was given to me at PCB. The love and encouragement I received from my professors put wind in my sails, and lifelong friendships were formed during those years.

The school was almost entirely white with a very small ethnic minority student population. After the first month or so, there were class elections; and one of my classmates put my name in the ring for class president. I didn't think I would win, but I had put together a team and we poured ourselves into the campaign. We were encouraged by what appeared to be momentum and growing support for our campaign. Perhaps my opponent didn't think that I was a serious threat, but I ended up winning the election by a sizeable margin. I was the first black president of any class in the history of the school.

The prominence of the civil rights movement and its impact on the country made this possible. Again, thank you, Dr. King.

I hadn't told my parents about the campaign. I suppose I was hedging my bets in case I lost. After the election I went home for the weekend. I couldn't wait to share the good news with my parents. I will never forget the look of astonishment on their faces. They were wonderfully surprised and happy for me. But there was something more I saw in their eyes. It was the glimmer of anticipation. In a small but significant way, they were saying, "Son, you have been given something that few in our generation experienced."

In fact, my mother said to me, "Now, Son, never forget where you came from." She wasn't throwing a cold blanket over my enthusiasm nor was she warning me about the dangers of abandoning my ethnic heritage. She was reminding me that I needed to remember with gratitude those who went before me and could not have this opportunity. In other words, I needed to greet this opportunity as a steward and with great humility. A necessary reminder for an eighteen-year-old!

Once elected to office I ran into something that I hadn't anticipated. It would be a preview of things to come for the next forty years, contributing to no small amount of frustration and pain. There is a loneliness that's associated with leadership. It goes with the territory, and it should be expected and anticipated. However, when that is compounded with the fact that you happen to be an ethnic minority in a predominantly white organization, it is not uncommon for other minorities to view you as having succumbed to some form of "white idolization." In other words, you have abandoned "us" and now you are with "them."

I sensed and felt this immediately when I became freshman class president. Some of my African American classmates pulled back from me. I found myself going out of my way to initiate conversations with them. It was as if they wanted me to make a choice. In my way of thinking, being class president was not choosing *any* side. I just wanted to do a good job at being class president.

Now all wasn't heaven on the "white side" of the ledger either. There were attempts to embarrass me by my opponents. For example, I wasn't familiar with *Roberts Rules of Order*. So in my attempt to lead our first official class meeting, I was butchered and humiliated by my opponents when they pointed out my many violations of that sacred guideline for running meetings. Was this racially motivated? I can't say for sure, but I strongly lean in that direction. By the way, after the meeting I bought a copy of *Roberts Rules of Order* and virtually memorized it. Lesson learned.

During my four years at PCB, I was involved in student government, sang in the college chorale, and toured with the college quar-
tet. The highlight of my college career was meeting Karen. We were
married at the end of my junior year and we've been married now
for forty-three years. My freshman year I joined the college chorale.
We sang on special occasions in chapel, performed in churches in the
area, and did an annual concert. The highlight of the year was the tour
to Florida during spring break. During the tour we sang in churches
around southern and central Florida. At the end of our concerts, we
would wait for the members of the church to come "claim" us for the
evening and we would enjoy a meal in a home, some good old Southern
hospitality, and a good night's rest.

One evening after the concert, one by one, all of the chorale members had been claimed by families of the church: all except me and
another young lady. We were the only black members of the chorale.
Imagine. As our friends one by one walked away chatting with their
hosts, I began thinking, "I hope this is not what it's beginning to look
like." It was. Even now as I write these words, I am revisited with the
feelings of self-consciousness and embarrassment. As I stood there
watching my friends leave and the church filing out, I began to feel the
shadow of rejection creeping over me. Finally a couple of the youth staff
"claimed" me and we spent the night at a youth camp outside of town.

The next day I found out what I already suspected. The folks in this
"fine Bible believing church" did not want a young black man sleeping
in their homes. Another version of the sign "Colored Served in Rear."
The hurt quickly turned to anger. I was incensed. I asked the chorale
director, "If I could sing in their church but wasn't good enough to
sleep in their homes, then why did you agree to sing in their church?"
Even at nineteen I knew that this was accommodating racism. When
we returned from tour, I quit the chorale.

It is this kind of sinful reflection of the culture that has given evangelicals a credibility problem. To be sure progress has been made, but many are still selective in the sins they choose to denounce. God chooses what is just and unjust. He is not obligated to select from the menu we offer Him. We will be held accountable for the whole counsel of God, including how we treat people.

I am thankful for that experience. It was a good old-fashioned dose of reality and, quite frankly, I needed that wake-up call. In perspective, it was nothing compared to what my parents and their generation had to swallow and put up with. I am so grateful to God that although I was very angry, I didn't get bitter and neither did it cause me to pull back from my white friends and the growing burden/vision for the visible expression of the unity of God's people across racial lines.

What also kept my reaction in check was the steadying influence of how I grew up and the very close friends I had who were white. I had eaten with them and slept in their homes and experienced their hospitality. I knew genuine love and inclusion from both black and white people. I could not deny nor dismiss their love and affection for me. This pulled me back from the cliff and protected me from blanket generalizations about all white people and all white Christians. In fact, in a strange way, I became even more determined to not allow what I was increasingly coming to recognize as "abnormal white Christians" to define who I would associate with and who I would love. If I did, I would be a victim and a casualty to their racism and their shortsighted brand of Christianity. By God's grace I couldn't let that happen. Thanks, again, Dr. King.

After four incredible years at PCB, it was time to move on. I had grown as a Christian and as a leader, and received increasing clarity concerning God's direction for my life. Although I have spent most of my ministry with parachurch organizations, including twenty-seven years on the staff of CRU (formerly Campus Crusade for Christ), I am and have always been (since age sixteen) a preacher. How well I do it is for others to judge, but I sense the presence, power, and pleasure of God when I proclaim His Word. I have had various leadership assignments through the years but I have never wandered far from this calling. But, as I've said, the context and "place setting" of this calling has been primarily within ethnically diverse and often predominantly white circles.

> **UNTIL WE COME to the place where we see ethnic diversity as more than a strategy, emphasis, or an occasional feature in our e-magazines, we will always be playing catch-up.**

In a very real sense, my generation was the first crop of the civil rights movement. It was an exciting time. The racial fabric of the country was changing, and compared to fifteen years earlier, more options and opportunities were open to African Americans. This included parachurch organizations, which for the most part had not made serious efforts at recruiting African Americans. Now they were faced with the need to respond to where things were headed and they had to get on board.

Looking back, this fills me with a bit of sadness. The church of Jesus Christ (I'm including parachurch agencies) should have been the prophetic, moral leader for justice and the reformation of society. Instead we were silent and waited for the government to take the initiative. Now, to be sure the Bible teaches that the government does exist for the well-being of the people; but too many Christians got lock-jaw, saying very little or nothing when in fact the country needed the engagement of the church and a word from God. Silence and business as usual did severe damage to our prophetic integrity. We've made progress but our efforts are still woefully inadequate.

Until we come to the place where we see ethnic diversity as more than a strategy, emphasis, or an occasional feature in our e-magazines ,we will always be playing catch-up. No, diversity has to be a core plank in the reason for the existence of our organizations.

I had gone to a predominantly white Christian college, and now it was time for me to start taking intentional steps toward the realization of the calling and vision God had placed on my heart. This was an exciting time for me but there were seasons in which I was visited with a sense of isolation and loneliness. I had a lot to learn (and I still do!). I was about to get a real education, and the vision on my heart was going to be challenged and tested.

With the exception of the two years I served with a church planting organization, targeting the black community, most of my ministry has been spent within the context of predominantly white Christian organizations. In fact, I was among a relatively small group of African Americans who had been recruited by parachurch organizations. We were called to do double duty. We felt the pressure to be the poster child for what these ministries were doing in and for the black community, and at the same time to educate our white peers in all things African American (from history to ebonics!). And, by the way, we needed to be effective and successful in our ministry assignments within those organizations. At times it was exasperating, answering the same questions over and over again, satisfying curiosity but not making big enough steps toward substantive change in behavior and attitudes.

This almost broke me. God used this pressure to carve something out of me that I needed to get rid of. It was a form of racism. Let me explain. From the time I was about ten or eleven years old, the way I proved myself when I was in predominantly white settings was to outperform them. This was not so much to gain their acceptance or approval but to put them in their place. I wanted to send a message: "You're not as good as you think you are, and you'd better take me seriously." Looking back this was a very strong drive in my early years.

This all started and was triggered by something Pop said to me when I was ten or eleven years old. I was playing Little League baseball and Pop wanted to give me a dose of reality. He said to me, "Son, when you're trying to make the team and you're going up against these white kids, you're going to have to be twice as good." He meant well and what he told me was particularly true at that time. But given my personality and bent, his words became a driving force in my life.

God had to teach me that it is not my job to put anybody in their place or to prove to anybody how valid, competent, and worthy black people are. I had to stop carrying stuff that God never meant for me to shoulder. I had to do my best because I was being faithful to the Lord and not trying to prove a point or send a message. God hammered away on me about this. But, bless His name, He set me free. It took tears, failures, and almost burnout to embrace the message.

I came to realize that this was a not so subtle form of racism and, in a weird way, a form of idolatry. It was sin and I needed to repent. If I was going to experience the fulfillment of the dream God had placed on my heart, then I needed to let God do it and stop being a roadblock to the very thing I desperately wanted to see God do. In this regard, the problem was not white people or black people. Crawford had to let God clean up his heart and motives.

Once I dealt with this I began to experience God's blessing and favor. I still faced heartache, challenges, and frustrations, but God forged in my heart a conviction that the only burden that I needed to carry was the one that God placed on my shoulders. And even that burden needed to be given back to Him.

Three Christian leaders who are towering figures in my life were the human instruments God used to shape, launch, and leverage the calling and vision that God placed on my heart. They didn't just give me opportunity, they loved me and did all they could to encourage me. They are white. Dr. Douglas MacCorkle (he was the president of PCB when I was a student), Olan Hendrix (the former general director of the American Missionary Fellowship and my first boss), and Dr. Bill Bright (the founder and president of Campus Crusade for Christ). And so I stop and pay each tribute. They were patient, kind, and loved me unconditionally. Their influence on my life, along with that of others, helped to give me balance and perspective as I faced some very challenging times. God placed these men in my life to point me toward what He wanted to do in and through me and to help translate vision to reality.

Nevertheless, being a "pioneer" is still lonely and at times expensive. As I served in the context of predominantly white settings, at times I felt out of sync with the expectations of many in the African American community. I was like the proverbial fish swimming up stream. The late 1960s and well into the decade of the 70s saw the celebration of our ethnicity. If you were "legitimately" black, then you were expected to show it and prove it. The black Christian community was no exception. You were expected to "come home," meaning to identify completely with the black community. The message was that it was a waste of time, education, and abilities to be ministering within a context that had more resources and opportunities than the black Christian community. So on many occasions my ethnic authenticity was called into question.

There's a not-so-very-nice expression used for those of us back then who were in these mainly white organizations, for now let's clean it up and call it "a house negro." Being accused of betraying my heritage hurt and hurt deeply. So, here you have it. Some of my white peers were asking, "Now, why are you here?" Likewise, black Christian friends were asking, "Now, why are you there?" Again, this was a painful, lonely time. I can't tell you the number of times I almost caved in and walked away.

But God wouldn't let me. Looking back, there were four things that helped me to stay the course. First, there was the concrete conviction that I was called by God to serve within a diverse context. Second, there was an ever-increasing clear vision that the integrity of the gospel demanded that the visible transformation of the power of Christ be demonstrated and modeled by the unity of the body of Christ. Third, in those moments in which I wanted to capitulate, I would hear the voice of my dad saying, "Boy, don't you ever let anybody tell you who your friends should be." Finally, love is powerful. I knew that Bill Tarr, Dennis Rainey, Josh McDowell, Steve Douglass, and a host of other colleagues whom I ministered alongside—who happened to be white—loved me and were committed to me. And besides, isn't this part of what Martin Luther King Jr. envisioned? Thank you, Dr. King.

I also found rich, wonderful encouragement from Tom Skinner. Tom was, in many respects, a prophetic voice calling all of evangelicalism, especially our white brothers, to live out the values of the kingdom of God. He spoke of becoming the just, reconciled people of God. His was a fresh voice of hope with which so many of us could identify. He offered a vision of inclusion anchored in the truth of the gospel that called the church to both face and repent of its racism. He spoke of any degree of racial exclusion as violating the integrity of the gospel.

This emphasis made many white evangelicals uncomfortable because it challenged the personal, privatized brand of Christianity that dominated the landscape of evangelicalism at the time. Some were fearful of anything that spoke of the church's corporate responsibility with regard to justice and the need to model the ethnic diversity of the gospel. Back then they were afraid to be labeled as proponents of the "social gospel" (an unfortunate carryover from the fundamentalist/liberal controversy that gave birth to modern evangelicalism).

Skinner believed that the white evangelical branch of the church needed to step forward and offer the transforming hope of the gospel to all of the issues facing us, including race and justice. For the most part, white evangelicals had been deafeningly silent throughout the civil rights struggle. Doesn't God have something to say about justice and freedom? Tom Skinner was relentless in this emphasis, speaking both with undeniable clarity and courage. And it cost him. He lost support but he never lost his message.

Tragically, Tom Skinner died at age fifty-two, a young man. So many of us stand on his shoulders. Not long ago I said to our son Bryan, "You know, today a lot of us say the very same things that Tom said with just as much passion and force and yet with nowhere near the reaction and push-back he got." In fact, I'm encouraged by the progress that's been made and the growing number of voices speaking for authentic reconciliation and justice. But it took men like Tom Skinner and John Perkins to stand in lonely places and speak and live hard, uncommon truth for God to get the attention of a frightened, accommodating church. The church of Jesus Christ, in these United States, owes these men a profound debt of gratitude. They, too, had been influenced by Martin Luther King Jr. Thank you, Dr. King.

> **I LOOK AT THESE young men and women and I confess the tears trickle down my cheeks and I bow in humble praise to God that He kept me from walking away from a calling that at times was painful and frustrating.**

These men inspired me to stay at it. Stick to the calling. See it through. So I have. I don't want to sound noble or unusual. I just want to finish what God called me to do. At this stage in my life, I realize that it's not about being successful, it's all about being faithful. I just want to finish my leg of the journey having been faithful to the vision and dream God placed on my heart. I want to be able to stand before my Savior and say I was a good steward of Your vision and dream for my moment in history.

Today I serve as the senior pastor of Fellowship Bible Church (FBC) in the Atlanta area. Demographically, we are a predominantly white church but growing in our ethnic diversity. I am the first African American pastor of our church. In fact the media thought that this was quite the story. I didn't think it was that big of a deal. I was fifty-five when I became their pastor, and by that time I had seen our great God tear down a lot of racial barriers along the way. I didn't come to FBC because I wanted to make a statement. I came to love the people and to preach the Word of God. In the process, and by God's amazing grace and enabling power, we are modeling the visible unity of the body of Christ and the hope and integrity of the gospel. We're not completely there yet, but we are moving in that direction with a shared sense of "holy impatience." Our leaders share the vision. We are called to be and do the will of God and not simply to clarify it and discuss it. We don't want to be known as a diverse church. We want to be known as the people of God. We will be diverse. I'm at FBC because of you, Dr. King. Thank you.

At sixty-four I'm thinking more about helping to influence and shape the next generation. Both of our sons are pastors and they lead ethnically diverse churches. We share the vision of modeling the kingdom. I find myself mentoring an ever-increasing group of this next generation who are called to live and minister in ethnically diverse contexts. I look at these young men and women and I confess the tears trickle down my cheeks, and I bow in humble praise to God that He kept me from walking away from a calling that at times was painful and frustrating.

Oh, the joy and the privilege of hearing them say in so many words, "We got it and we will take it from here." I don't feel as alone and out of sync as I did in those early years. I don't struggle with questions like,

"Have I abandoned my people?" or "Do they think I'm too white or too black?" I've concluded that at a point those are superficial, unnecessary questions. I can appreciate my heritage and love all people, especially my brothers and sisters in Christ. Who says we have to make a choice? God has given us the joy, privilege, and power to do both.

There's a gospel song that is dear to me. In dark, lonely times I have found myself singing and rehearsing these words: "I don't feel no ways tired . . . I've come too far from where I've started from . . . Nobody told me that the road would be easy . . . I don't believe you've brought me this far to leave me."

Thank you, Crawford and Sylvia, for paying my tuition. By God's grace I didn't drop out of school.

Thank you, Dr. King, for staying the course. You are helping me to finish mine. We've come a long way, but we have quite a ways to go . . .

Dear Dr. King,

My life has been indirectly impacted by your ministry, as your response to the racial tensions during your time helped shaped my parents and their ideologies.

In your Birmingham letter you spoke of "white brothers in the South who have grasped the meaning of social revolution and committed themselves to it." You said, "They are few in quantity, but they are big in quality . . . they have recognized the urgency of the moment and sensed the need for powerful "action" antidotes to combat the disease of segregation." Reading these words, I think about my parents.

Exposure to those racial tensions motivated them to raise my siblings and me in a diverse environment as a bold and direct action against racism and injustice. I was privileged to grow up in this unique environment.

I thought that I was well-versed in diversity, but I discovered in seminary that there was much to be learned as I talked with my African-American brothers about race, justice, and the gospel. Taking the posture of a learner, I benefited from their rebukes and encouragement as they "schooled" me, helping me see that racial ignorance is a luxury of the majority culture.

Today I minister with these same brothers. We are moving forward, united. While the church has much to do in the way of change, none of us wants to be guilty of doing it again: remaining silent when a brother is in need. Turning a blind eye to injustice when a brother's dignity is threatened. Asking a brother to wait when his very life is at stake.

We are intentional in our actions and words, as we war against all that hinders God's kingdom and its fullest expression.

Thank you for the legacy of Christian service you have passed on to us. I'm exceedingly grateful.

Pastor John Bryson

4

DON'T DO IT AGAIN

John Bryson

IT WAS A HOT, steamy Saturday afternoon, humidity so thick you could almost choke on it. The year was 1948. My mother, who was ten years old at the time, and her fourteen-year-old sister were coming home from a glorious day trip to Main Street in downtown Memphis, Tennessee. The sights, sounds, snow cones, departments stores, hustle and bustle were just about heaven for two young sisters from Capleville, located in southeast Memphis, just north of the Mississippi state line. My mother and aunt had made this trip often, but what happened on the way home on this particular day would forever haunt my mother and forever change the trajectory of her life.

This was the South and during the days of segregation, so when these two young ladies boarded the bus for the ride home, they turned and sat in the front row of the "white section" of the bus. As my mother tells the story, they were the only two whites on the bus. There were between eight and ten empty rows in the white section. And the black section of the bus was packed. As the bus coughed exhaust and rumbled east on Lamar Avenue, it came to a stop, and a black man got on. He headed toward the back of the bus, saw there were no seats available, and plopped down in what technically was the last row of the white section. What happened next still feels like slow motion for my mother sixty years later. The bus driver got up, grabbed a club, walked back, hit the man six times, and threw him off the bus.

I did not witness those events but it is still hard for me to write about it. I cannot imagine the anger, fear, or the physical and emotional pain that man experienced. The horror, shame, and guilt stayed with my mother. It left her feeling horrible for the man and like it was her fault.

Fast-forward fifteen years and my parents are driving north, headed to start a life and family with Memphis in their rear view mirror. They longed to find a place to raise their kids away from all the racial strife and tension they had experienced in Memphis. That same strife and tension would soon spill over into the sanitation strikes and would lead to the murder of Dr. Martin Luther King Jr. on the balcony of the Memphis Lorraine Motel.

After several years in Michigan, where my father did a residency in ophthalmology, my parents settled in a small mountain town in eastern Kentucky. As they settled in Harlan in 1969, my parents made a pledge to themselves that would be considered bold now and was for sure bold in 1969; they would not give their energies to anything that was not interracial, interdenominational, and offering life change through Jesus. They wanted to intentionally raise their kids in an environment of diversity and go to war against racism. They wanted to be unifiers and reconcilers. And they wanted a new normal for their kids.

RELATIONSHIP

In one of her first weeks in her new Kentucky town, my mother went to an evening church service. An African American lady shared her journey with cancer and sang a song. As Shirley Raglin was sharing and singing, the Spirit of God impressed upon my mother this phrase, "She is your sister." "She is your sister." My mother was not quite sure what to do with that leading, but she found herself knocking on Shirley's door later that week and being welcomed into her home.

Shirley was the wife of James Raglin, pastor of the largest African-American church in our town, and the mother of seven children. Her body was being ravaged by cancer and constant medical treatments. My mother came alongside her at this time and their friendship was birthed in the soil of my mother cooking meals for Shirley, helping her clean her home, and helping her with the laundry. The two of them shared stories, shared life, and prayed together. In the early and mid-1970s people from both communities in our small town were intrigued and amazed that this black family and white family shared meals together, were in each other's homes, and did life together.

I grew up in that unique environment. It was a precious gift to me. I remember the Raglins' home as well as I remember my own. That friendship opened up many more friendships across racial and cultural lines and took our family on an amazing journey of learning, healing, understanding, respect, admiration, and love.

AS A TEN-YEAR-OLD, I was now part of a racially and culturally mixed family. Race entered my life and blessed; race also entered and hurt.

In 1978, Shirley died of cancer and left Pastor Jim with seven kids, all under eighteen years of age. Shirley had asked my parents in her final days if they would take into our family her two youngest, Darrin and Shana. As a ten-year-old, I was now part of a racially and culturally mixed family. Race entered my life and blessed; race also entered and hurt. Months after Darrin and Shana had become a part of our family, several matriarchs of the African American community voiced a concern that it was wrong for black children to be raised by white parents. They confronted my mother, and in a heart-wrenching decision she still questions to this day, Darrin and Shana left our home.

Reconciliation and bridge building is messy, be it organizationally, culturally, or relationally. It is not for the faint of heart. There are tough calls and it can often feel like three steps forward and two steps back. Perseverance is crucial.

DISPLACEMENT

As an overflow of our family relationship with the Raglins, I found myself living my life in and out of both the black community and white community in our little town. I thought nothing of being the only white person on a youth trip with Pastor Raglin's church or at his church's state convention. I spent many evenings in the Raglins' home and later in the home of Fred Fluker. God gave me the gift of displacement as a young child. And I've learned that this is an essential for any majority culture person who wishes to be a reconciler.

Displacement is the experience of being in a culture not your own. Most minorities in America experience displacement every day. Many majority culture men and women never experience displacement. For those who do experience it, they discover that it can be disorienting, uncomfortable, and even frightening. It can also be powerfully redemptive and even great fun, if you experience it humbly, as a learner, with respect, and not ridicule or judgment.

FRIENDSHIP

The first birthday and Christmas gifts I ever received from someone not family were from Fred Fluker, an African American who went to school with me and was eleven years old at the time. Fred was the first person outside of my family to love me, at least that I noticed. We became best friends in elementary school, both got to be managers for the high school football team (a big deal for a fourth and a fifth grader!), and stayed tight all the way through high school and into college. We ran around together, stayed in each other's homes, took road trips together, played ball together, bought the first Jordan's together (he got the red, white, and black; I got the red and black), went to summer camps together, went to concerts together (Run DMC!), and because of another strategic move by my parents, we got to experience a children's and youth ministry together.

INTENTIONALITY

Intentionality is a nonnegotiable for those with a heart for reconciliation. Harlan, Kentucky, in the 1970s and 1980s, was as segregated along church lines as everywhere else. I'm writing this forty years later and what Dr. King wrote in the 1960s "11 o'clock on Sunday morning is still the most segregated hour in America" still rings true. In the midst of a divided church culture, my mother began an after-school ministry/program for elementary school kids called the Thursday Afternoon Program and a ministry for the junior high and high school kids in our community on Saturday nights called the Saturday Night Group. These ministries served all children, regardless of race or economic background.

A few years ago in celebration of my parents' fiftieth wedding anniversary, we honored them with a reunion of that Saturday Night Group. Men and women drove from hundreds of miles to reassemble in a church basement to remember God's grace toward us as kids and teenagers and the wildly unique privilege of being in a racially and socioeconomically diverse children's and youth ministry.

DIVERSITY

I started college in the fall of 1987. Though there is no physical or photographic evidence, I think I had two lines ala Vanilla Ice shaved into the right side of my head and three swatches, with guards, on my left wrist. I promise it was cool. I think. At Asbury, a small, liberal arts college in central Kentucky, I experienced a new kind of diversity. The student body of roughly twelve hundred students was made up of collegians from forty-eight different states and seventeen countries. It was fascinating to hear people's stories, how they grew up, and what life was like in other parts of the country and on other continents of the world. Though the school was in Kentucky, there were way more non-Kentuckians than Kentuckians that made up the student body. I was often teased about my accent in my own state. I'd always reply the same way, "You are in my state; you have the accent!"

After college I moved to Denton, Texas, to take part in a discipleship program with a pastor named Tom Nelson. He took twelve of us and met with us four mornings a week in his living room. He started in Genesis and taught us the historical books of the Old Testament. He opened each morning with a proverb, encouraged us not to be an idiot, and then taught us God's Word. I started serving with the college ministry first as an intern, then as part-time staff, and eventually became the college pastor at Denton Bible Church in 1995. Both the church and college ministry were predominately white, though the town of Denton and for sure the University of North Texas were incredibly diverse.

POSTURE: LEARNER

Though my experiences had been diverse throughout my first twenty-five years of life, my thinking about race, the gospel, and church—my racial IQ if you will—was typical for a majority culture, white American . . . pitifully low. It used to be true of me and is true for most of my white brothers and sisters in Christ. We can talk on college and graduate school levels when it comes to issues of justification, sanctification, ecclesiology, soteriology, etc., but when it comes to issues of the gospel and race, sadly and embarrassingly, many of us stumble and bumble like first graders. Racial ignorance is a luxury of the majority culture. We really must be willing to place ourselves in the posture of a learner.

God used a number of influencers to shape my thinking about race. Through my relationships with D'hati Lewis and James Roberson, another African American who had come to study in Denton, I was led into great discussions and honest conversations about race, the gospel, and the church. Another major influence was James White, an African American who mentored me.

I'm so thankful for men like Eric Mason, Bryan Loritts, and many others who have continued to press into me on issues of the gospel, race, and the church. I'm so glad these men had the courage to be honest with me, challenge me, rebuke me, and force me to learn. I remember late nights, sitting in a booth in "The Cup" in Denton, Texas, getting a flat-out education from James Roberson on race. James helped me understand terms and phrases like majority culture, white privilege, and the ridiculous position of "color blindness" that, sadly, so many majority culture men and women hold on to as a virtue!

I'm so glad that George Yancey has written all he has written on the subject of racial reconciliation, and that Bryan Loritts had our staff team in the early days of Fellowship Memphis read books like James Baldwin's *The Fire Next Time*, W. E. B Dubois's *The Souls of Black Folk*, and a biography of Malcolm X. Taking the posture of a learner, engaging in friendships with people different from me, and reading history and various perspectives has been a grace to me and has grown me in incredible ways. I'm not where I want to be when it comes to my "Racial IQ," but by becoming a learner and exposing myself to relationships and books, I am making good progress. As my posture of learning has increased my "Racial IQ," it has only furthered my heart and passion to be a unifier and racial reconciler.

SEGREGATED CHURCH BECOMES GLARING

During my first few years as a college pastor, our college ministry began to grow by leaps and bounds. From 1995 to 2000 the ministry grew from one hundred to almost one thousand students. Evidences of God's grace were everywhere, but a deep tension was growing in me.

The University of North Texas was actually majority-minority (like California and Texas, and soon, America), but our college ministry was predominately white. I wanted to take steps to diversify, but I did not know what steps to take.

D'hati Lewis joined our staff and the two of us worked together to reach our campus, but the glaringness of us having two college ministries—one primarily white and the other primarily black—was starting to become unexplainable. I understood it from a minority perspective, but grieved it from a majority perspective. I grieved that we had not been intentional in creating a climate conducive to all from the beginning. I was sad that we had not incorporated minority leadership from the inception and allowed them to share in key decisions and speak into who we were and what we did as a ministry. I decided that if I ever had the chance to start a ministry or business or organization from scratch, I'd be intentional about making sure diversity was in its DNA and minority leadership at all the decision-making tables would be a nonnegotiable.

It is incredible to look back now and see all that God was stirring in those waters of the college town of Denton. It was there that Lecrae came to Christ and met Ben Washer (a white guy) and together formed Reach Records. Michael "Stew" Steward got his leadership start that would blossom into a diversified "Verge" movement. Dave Furman got a vision for the nations and went on to plant a church in the middle of Dubai. Little did we know that our "wrestling" in those days would bear fruit a decade later.

WE ARE DOING IT AGAIN

I remember having scattered thoughts as a twentysomething leader, and thinking that once leaders from my generation got into their thirties and forties and into positions of leadership in the church, segregated church would quickly go away. Gen Xers, or whatever we were called—those of us not alive when Dr. King was shot, those of us who didn't live in the thick of the civil rights movement, those of us who did not experience firsthand segregated schools or businesses —surely we would lead the diversity revolution. I'll never forget a Wednesday night in October 2003 outside of Atlanta at a conference rallying "next generation leaders" and being in an arena, listening to Coldplay worship, and looking around at basically twelve thousand white twenty- and thirtysomethings. I looked around and thought, "We are gonna do it again!"

TRANSITIONS

During my tenth year with the college ministry of Denton Bible Church, in 2002, God began to stir my heart toward church planting. I was graced with a three-month sabbatical by Denton Bible Church and used that time to rest, recover, and think about the future. I had always felt my ability to connect with college students was on a clock that was ticking. So I sought advice on what I should be thinking about regarding the next decade of my life from a few mentors, including my boss and senior pastor of Denton Bible Church, Tom Nelson. Each affirmed in me a love for the church, a leadership gift, and recognized me as an entrepreneur; those three things seemed to collide into church planting.

MEMPHIS

As God often does when He has guided me over the years, He confirms His will in a variety of ways. When I read a *World Magazine* article making the argument that the "Worst Cities" were the best places for a gospel presence (Memphis ranked the fourth worst city to live in that particular year), it all seemed to point to MEMPHIS! That's where we are going. We were going to Memphis to love a city and beg God to create a church. A church that looked like Memphis, in all it's beautiful diversity.

Memphis is growing out of a well-earned inferiority complex. It was positioned in the 1800s to be a major city of the Midwest with populations higher than Chicago, St Louis, and Dallas until a plague called yellow fever, carried by mosquitoes, slaughtered the swampy city. Many were killed. Many more moved. It took Memphis a century to recover. Then in the mid-1900s Memphis was positioned, because of its prime location on the mighty Mississippi River and its delta surroundings with a plethora of cotton, to be a major Southern city. It had a future brighter than Charlotte, Atlanta, and Nashville. Then came the nightmare of the murder of Dr. Martin Luther King Jr—in the words of Bono, "early morning, April 4, shot rang out in the Memphis sky."

The next thirty years would see Charlotte, Atlanta, and Nashville boom, while Memphis struggled to survive. The fact that we chose Memphis to plant our church, our families, and our lives resonated deeply with Memphians. We have found that if you love Memphis, Memphis will love you back! We believed that if a multiracial church could happen in Memphis, the second most segregated city in America, miles from where Dr. King was assassinated, Jesus would be massively glorified, and it would remove excuses from every other city.

FELLOWSHIP MEMPHIS

We knew a year before actually moving to Memphis that Memphis was where we were going to plant a church. We had deep desires to see the gospel work itself out in such a way—both in our church and in our city—that racial healing happened. We begged God in our prayers to make us a church family made up of people across racial, cultural, ethnic, generational, and socioeconomic lines. We wanted the gospel to bring together what humanity so frequently segregates.

At that point we had vision, but very little strategy to attempt to make that vision a reality. I felt deeply that a diverse church would not happen apart from diversity in our leadership from the beginning. We began to pray for diversity in our leadership, launch team, and in our church. Two white guys (Ben Parkinson and I) and an Asian American (Tony Kim) started looking for an African American with gifts of leadership and preaching to move to Memphis and labor with us.

I called four mentors and asked them this question, "Who is the best under forty leader and preacher you know of in the church world?" All four mentioned the name Bryan Loritts. I'll never forget the day I called Bryan. I was actually visiting Memphis, driving north on East Parkway. (It's a Memphis thing. East Parkway goes north and south while North Parkway goes east and west.) I called Bryan out of the blue and said something along the lines of "Man, you do not know me, but we have a crazy dream to plant a church in Memphis and I think you need to be a part of it. Please do not tell me no, now. At least let me fly to Charlotte and tell you about it. Give me one afternoon." For some reason, he said yes. A couple of days later, Ben Parkinson and I were on a plane.

ICE STORMS AND TEAMMATES

Our plane landed almost sideways and the sleet was pounding us as we ran to get a rental car. What should have been a ten-minute trip became three hours as the roads got worse and worse. We part slid, part parked into Bryan's driveway, and our afternoon conversation turned into a three-day marathon of ice, snow, theology, ministry philosophy, Play Station 2, job descriptions, stories, and Bryan laughing at having to dig a fan out of the attic for me to have beside my bed in twenty-degree weather. When we left we were not sure if the Lord would lead and guide Bryan to join us; but a few months later, Memorial Day weekend of 2003, we all moved to Memphis.

CHURCH PLANTING

I will spare you all the joy and pain of the early years of church planting. Raising money, recruiting a launch team, getting vision down on paper, creating doctrinal statements, building relationships, looking for places to meet, looking for places to office, everything to do and nothing to do; it peaks every emotion and surfaces every idol.

Church planting seemed difficult enough, adding to our vision a body that would be a family of rich and poor, young and old, black, white and other seemed incredibly daunting and incredibly right! We had no idea how to do this and could not, not do this. We cried out to the Lord for help and He answered.

THE GOD OF ALL PEOPLES

I believe from Genesis to Revelation that God is the God of all nations and all peoples. He created all things, including all peoples, all people groups, all races, and all skin colors. From the beginning of the Bible to the end of the Bible, you see God redeeming all people to Himself. John 3:16 tells us God sent Jesus because "God so loved the world." The Acts of the Apostles tells the story of the earliest church plants. The gospel-dominated people of Matthew, Mark, Luke, and John spilled over into the launching of gospel communities, or church plants in Acts. Racial and cultural issues surfaced almost immediately. Jesus had actually been the one to begin stirring this pot in His ministry as He intentionally went to Samaria, and did all sorts of things with and for Gentiles that Jewish men were not supposed to do.

As early as Acts 6 an issue arose in the church concerning the neglect of the Hellenistic widows. The Jewish widows were cared for while the culturally Greek, Jewish widows were not. Side note: I am so glad that the early apostles did not start a separate Hellenistic church or service to deal with the issues in the Hellenistic, widow community!

A GOSPEL ISSUE

By Acts 10 and 11, Peter, a racial, ethnic, and cultural Jew, was struggling with this whole new Jesus vision of a church that included

Jews and Gentiles. Jesus helped him by giving him a dream that let him know that in this "new normal" Peter could eat Gentile food. He began reaching toward relating to, ministering to, and eating with Gentiles. Pass the ribs! (I choose to believe Rendevzous Ribs was planted between Acts 8 and Acts 9, but I may be off.) Then some of his old friends called Peter on it, questioned him about this practice, and Peter, forgetting the gospel, slipped back into old racial habits and stopped fellowshipping with Gentiles. It is fascinating to me and a game changer how Paul confronts Peter over this decision.

> But when Cephas came to Antioch, I opposed him to his face, because he stood condemned. For before certain men came from James, he was eating with the Gentiles; but when they came he drew back and separated himself, fearing the circumcision party. And the rest of the Jews acted hypocritically along with him, so that even Barnabas was led astray by their hypocrisy. But when I saw that their conduct was not in step with the truth of the gospel, I said to Cephas before them all, "If you, though a Jew, live like a Gentile and not like a Jew, how can you force the Gentiles to live like Jews?" (Galatians 2:11–14)

IT IS INCONSISTENT with the gospel for believers to lift up the name of Jesus with one hand and hold on to racial attitudes, thoughts, beliefs, or actions in the other hand.

Bam! ". . . their conduct was not in step with the truth of the gospel." Paul here makes issues of race, culture, and favoritism at its core a gospel issue. It is inconsistent with the gospel for believers to lift up the name of Jesus with one hand and hold on to racial attitudes, thoughts, beliefs, or actions in the other hand. The gospel will dominate a person and part of the reconstruction of that person will be a reorienting of our view of everything, including race.

PETER'S RACIAL GROWTH

In light of this Acts incident and Galatians confrontation by Paul, it adds even more volume to what Peter himself would later write in 1 Peter 2:9–10:

> But you are a chosen race, a royal priesthood, a holy nation, a people for his own possession, that you may proclaim the excellencies of him who called you out of darkness into his marvelous light. Once you were not a people, but now you are God's people; once you had not received mercy, but now you have received mercy.

How is that for gospel and racial growth in the life of Peter! He now describes gospel-transformed people as a "chosen race." One race. A new race. Peter argues the gospel replaces my race, culture and ethnicity as the primary identifier of my life.

THE REVELATION OF JESUS

John's vision of heaven in both Revelation 5 and 7 mentions seeing a great multitude of people from every tongue, tribe, nation, and language. Heaven's description includes nice meals, great parties, and worship of God. I believe in those Revelation moments when we are having meals and parties together, and people from every tongue, tribe, nation, and people group are singing songs together to the King of Kings and Lord of Lords. We are not going to care whether we are singing an Israel Houghton song, a Chris Tomlin song, or a John Wesley song. I believe we are not going to care if we are accompanied by a Hammond B-3, an acoustic guitar, an organ, or a jug (shout out to Kentucky). Why? Because the object of our worship will so consume us, the means through which we worship is secondary at best. If you do not like the diverse church, you are going to hate heaven.

WHITE PRIVILEGE

We live in an incredibly racialized society and most of my white brothers and sisters are oblivious to issues of race. Even as our country's population trends toward a majority-minority population, power structures, boardrooms, leadership positions, and wealth are deeply tilted toward whites and always have been in our country. Our white ancestors structured laws to make sure of that. As one author notes, "America was stolen from one people and built on the backs of another people." Ugly parts of American history need to be owned, acknowledged, and ought to lead us to ask for forgiveness and repent (Nehemiah models that for us).

> **DON'T JUST WISH your organization was diverse: do something about it.**

I beg my white brother and sisters to not only be honest about history but repent of any racial tendencies that rise within them. Every Christian is a recovering racist to one degree or another. But there is more. Way more. Go on a mission to step out of racial ignorance and raise your racial IQ. Pursue relationships with people different from you who will talk deeply and honestly with you about issues of race. Wrestle deeply with how you might steward your white privilege for the benefit of others. Put yourself and your kids in places where they are "displaced." Place yourself under minority leadership. Educate yourself on the veiled racial code that has become the norm (the dark side of "political correctness") and on systemic issues of injustice. Strive beyond "I'm not a racist" to become an "antiracist."

And finally, if you are a fellow brother in church leadership, church planting, or in organizational leadership, please develop a theology of race. Please relate deeply with minorities and those different from you. A diverse life precedes a diverse organization or church. You cannot reproduce what you are not. Please allow minority leaders into positions of power with you to make decisions for and speak into whatever is being created or led. Don't just wish your organization was diverse: do something about it.

Please read deeply and widely on issues of race. Please read authors of color. Become a learner. Understand the consequences of being in the majority culture. It dupes us into believing that our normal is normal, and worse, makes us a judge of any cultural differences that are different from our own. Please stop thinking there is one black opinion on things, one Hispanic position, one Asian way of thought, etc. There are millions of people in every people group with millions of positions, ideas, reasons for doing things.

I need grace when it comes to the gospel and race. We all need grace. God help us.

Dear Dr. King,

Since your time, we've seen change. In our age of diversity and tolerance, hate groups have been pushed to society's margins; schools have become integrated; and blacks have voting rights among a number of other privileges not afforded in your day. We've also seen the emergence of strong black men and women who are eating the fruit of prosperity because of you and the generation of marchers who suffered so we could live with a greater sense and degree of dignity.

Reflecting on your letter, I am drawn to your commentary about the indifference and passivity of the white moderate who pleaded with you to "slow down and wait" and criticized you for being "religiously in a hurry" while black men hung as strange fruit from Southern trees. While many things have changed, there are some things that to a degree remain the same.

I believe that as we move forward, toward the future, we do so still fighting indifference and passivity. This is evident in the pleas of our Christian brothers who ask children of the oppressed to just preach the gospel instead of addressing social issues such as racial and economic inequality.

In many ways, I have stubbed my toe against this brick of passivity most of my life. Thankfully, God has used these painful moments to break, heal, and grow me in my service to Him and others.

Your desire was to see that old brick of passivity toppled in the name of Jesus Christ. It's also my desire. As I engage Christian brothers to see the body of Christ unified and more multiethnic churches born, I do so believing that living together on one accord, we will see this brick removed for good.

Thank you for your persistence.

Carrying the Cross,

Pastor Bryan Loritts

5

WHY WE CAN'T WAIT FOR THE MULTIETHNIC CHURCH

Bryan Loritts

READING MARTIN Luther King Jr's "Letter from a Birmingham Jail," one cannot help but feel his passion. Finding every scrap of paper he could, Dr. King stretched his arms through those cell bars and grabbed a nation by the lapels urgently inviting us to join the fight against injustice. King's passion was fueled by the ironic and tragic demands of white clergy who begged him to be patient. Like pouring gasoline on a fire, the passivity of his colleagues only served to further enflame Dr. King's quest for equality.

It is easy to confuse King's philosophy of nonviolence as being the natural extension of a docile man, but if one sees King as that naïve sheep being led to the slaughter, you should look again. There are times, in fact, when King appeared to be annoyed, impatient, and nothing triggered his annoyance faster than having his heels nipped at by one of his own, begging this "drum major for justice" to slow his pace. He seems to lose it outright when he states:

> I must make two honest confessions to you, my Christian and Jewish brothers. First, I must confess that over the last few years I have been gravely disappointed with the white moderate. I have almost reached the regrettable conclusion that the Negro's great stumbling block is not the White Citizens

Counciler or the Ku Klux Klanner, but the white moderate who is more devoted to 'order' than to justice, who prefers a negative peace which is the absence of tension to a positive peace which is the presence of justice, who constantly says 'I agree with you in the goal you seek, but I can't agree with your methods of direct action,' who paternalistically believes that he can set the timetable for another man's freedom. [1]

King was not most put off by burning crosses, biting dogs, or the thunderous explosions of water being turned on little kids marching in the streets. What agitated him the most was the indifference of his seminary trained, gospel preaching colleagues, who wanted King to just slow down for a moment while black men continued to hang as "strange fruit" from Southern trees. Given the nature of his relationship with the Jewish Rabbi Abraham Joshua Heschel, who accompanied King in his quest for equality, one cannot help but conclude that as Dr. King wrote this letter he had Heschel's words pounding in the back of his head that the only thing worse than the evil of injustice is indifference.

THE BRICK OF PASSIVITY

By all accounts it would seem as if Jim Crow—the American system of apartheid—has been demolished, completely eradicated from society. The images of Birmingham in 1963 have been relegated to the pages of history and the halls of antiquity. In an age of diversity and tolerance, hate groups such as the Ku Klux Klan have been pushed so far to the margins of society that they are detested even by their own ethnicity. Our schools have become integrated; and a voting rights and civil rights act have been signed securing a whole new way of life for blacks in this country. While poverty, crime, and incarceration continue to plague the black community in disproportionate amounts, serving as a reminder that we still have more work to do, what cannot be ignored is the emergence of a strong black middle to upper-middle class who have "moved on up to the east side." For black men like me who are eating the fruit of prosperity, we owe Dr. King, Reverend Ralph Abernathy, John Lewis, and a whole generation of marchers (and more) who literally suffered so that we might live in a fair and just society.

But there is one last brick that remains from the statue of old man Jim Crow. It is the same brick that King tried to topple in his opus, "Letter from a Birmingham Jail." He labored with all of his might but could never pull it out from Jim's edifice. It is the brick of passivity. The same indifference and passivity that prompted Southern clergy to beg King to take his time is the same indifference we continue to fight today among so many who name the name of Jesus Christ.

What exactly do I mean when I talk of passivity, especially when it comes from the ranks of some of my beloved evangelical friends and colleagues? It's the kind of response that begs the children of the oppressed to just preach the gospel instead of addressing social issues such as racial and economic inequality—as if the latter is not a part of the former.

I have been stubbing my toe against the brick of passivity all of my life. I grew up in the home of two loving parents who shared and modeled what it means to follow Jesus Christ authentically. My father and mother served on the staff of a very large, prominent, white Christian organization that was committed to proclaiming the gospel. One of the primary venues this ministry utilized to accomplish their objective was to host large conferences of college students from various regions. As a little boy I remember traveling with my father to hear him address these gatherings. There I was at eight or nine years of age at a Christian conference, and I was acutely aware that I was different. The style of music was a far cry from what we sang at the small black Baptist church we attended. My father was the only African American on the program for the whole week, and looking around at a crowd of about a thousand, I could always count on one hand the people who looked like me.

What's more is that as I got older both my discomfort and curiosity only grew. How could this be, especially in cities like Atlanta where there were many historically black colleges and universities? Why weren't they represented in masse at these gatherings? Why was nothing being done from a music and speaking standpoint to communicate from the stage Paul's understanding of the gospel: that it is for the Jews *and* the Greeks (Romans 1:16)?

BIBLE COLLEGE

My frustration only grew when I entered the halls of Bible college in the fall of 1991. Through an intense sequence of events, God had clearly called me into vocational ministry, and I enrolled in this school desiring to be equipped for a lifetime of fruitful ministry. Yet as I sat in preaching classes, there was this pervasive feeling that something was missing. Why were all of the examples of great preachers white? Praise God for Charles Spurgeon, D. Martyn Lloyd-Jones, and Charles Swindoll; but why no mention of Gardner Taylor, E. V. Hill, or E. K. Bailey? How was I to interpret this oversight?

> **I DON'T KNOW what it's like to have German shepherds unleashed on you in the streets of Birmingham, but I do know the feeling of anonymity one has as he takes his seat in the halls of white evangelicalism.**

It was easy for me to conclude that the silent ignoring of people of color meant that great preaching is white, and that my professors did not care enough to be more inclusive in their curriculum. When I would politely question their omission, their response was laced with passive indifference.

Chapel service only served to further substantiate my thesis. The vast majority of chapel preachers were white. African American preachers were featured maybe once or twice a year. I remember once going to the professor who directed our chapel program and asking for more African American representation. His response was that, while he would love to, his fear was that they would be too emotional. What he was looking for were men who handled the text, were real expositors of the Bible, and were not driven by feelings.

As far as I can tell, I was never discriminated against in college. However, I did feel a nonexistence like what Ralph Ellison described in his groundbreaking book, *Invisible Man*. Ellison's depiction of the black man in the era of Jim Crow is masterful. The lead character has no name. Why would it matter if he had a name when all he's known as is *boy* or some racial slur? Ellison's point is that identity doesn't matter when you don't even have a place at the table. It is the inhumanity of anonymity. I don't know what it's like to have German shepherds unleashed on you in the streets of Birmingham, but I do know the feeling of anonymity one has as he takes his seat in the halls of white evangelicalism. It didn't take me long to figure out that I was Ellison's *Invisible Man*.

LAKE AVENUE CHURCH

You stub your toe against the brick of passivity long enough and you'll get angry, very angry. It's a matter of deep shame for me to have to confess that my experiences with my white brothers and sisters in places like my Bible college worked in me a deep-seated hatred of whites. Four years earlier I had entered Bible college with the hopefulness of Dr. King, but now on graduation day I was exiting with the vitriol of Malcolm X. I needed a respite from whites, a permanent one, or so I thought.

I spent the next three years rehabilitating in the black church. In my mind I thought this was where I would spend the rest of my ministry years serving. Here, amidst the sea of blacks, and the choruses of choirs bellowing out verses that resonated with the substance and style of my soul, I exhaled the sigh of relief of some vagabond who had finally crossed the threshold of home. I thought I could deal with my hatred by simply forgetting, but little did I realize it was merely buried deep in the inner chambers of my heart. God was about to deal with me.

Two events happened in my third year at Faithful Central Bible Church that would alter the trajectory of my life. The first is that I met and fell in love with the woman who is now my bride, Korie Benavides Loritts. As her maiden name suggests, she is *not* black. Now I would be less than honest if I were to tell you that I was dead set on marrying a black woman, but I am a man first who has always treasured a deep appreciation for a beautiful woman regardless of her ethnicity, and Korie represents God's finest work. I was compelled to ask her out. *God, what are You doing*? I thought, as I fell madly in love with this half Irish, half Mexican woman? Little did I know that the same God who had Peter live with a tanner, and then tell him to eat nonkosher food so that he could take the gospel to a Gentile's house, was the same God who was setting me up for a future ministry assignment that would change my life.

During the time I was falling in love with Korie, a white church in Pasadena approached me to join their staff as the first African American in their one hundred-plus-years history. God made it clear that this was my next ministry assignment. So in July of 1998, I moved into my office there at 393 North Lake Avenue kicking and screaming, much the same way the Jewish prophet Jonah came walking into the Gentile town of Nineveh. I felt like God had called me to pastor a people whom I did not like.

One of my first meetings was with an eighty-six-year-old man named Evan who graciously invited me to breakfast. Looking back I don't recall much about our conversation as we sat across from one another in a booth at Co-Co's on Lake Avenue. But what I do remember are three words this octogenarian white man said to me, "I love you." There was a sweetness to his spirit and an authenticity to his demeanor that made me believe him. Those three words reached down into me and did something. For the first time in my life, I felt as if I had leaped from the pages of Ellison's novel and had a name among my white brothers and sisters. In Evan's own way he said that I mattered. Immediately I excused myself from the table, went to the restroom, and had a good cry.

The next three years at Lake Avenue Church were redemptive for me. It felt as if someone had hit defrost on the dashboard of my heart. Neither time, nor the purposes of this essay, permits me to thank the dear people of Lake Avenue Church who God used as the balm in Gilead to begin to eradicate the bitterness I had toward whites. But I would do an injustice if I didn't thank the gentleman who was senior pastor of Lake Avenue at that time, Dr. Gordon Kirk. There I was, twenty-five years of age, and Dr. Kirk made it a point to share his pulpit with me. In an era where terms like "team teaching" were unknown, Dr. Kirk decided to transition the church in this direction, and the man he decided to have as his copilot was me, a twenty-five-year-old black man.

We taught together on the most important day of the Christian calendar, Resurrection Sunday. And I remember one sermon series we did together on spiritual gifts. When it came time to preach on the gift of tongues, Dr. Kirk handed me the keys to the car so to speak, and told me that he wanted me to guide his six thousand-plus-member church through this difficult subject. I can still see the grin on his face as he said that he trusted me. He would go on to give me the Sunday evening service, and to become my biggest cheerleader. Dr. Kirk was just another of God's team of physicians there at Lake to restore my wounded spirit. If it had not been for those dear, proactive (not passive) white men and women, I would never have made it to Memphis to plant a multiethnic church.

LABOR PAINS

It was during my time at Lake Avenue that God began to open doors to preach the gospel to the broader body of Christ. My travels found me standing before homogenous audiences, and as I preached the gospel of that Great Reconciler to all black, or all white audiences, I began to wonder when we were going to ever come together? This righteous angst reached a crescendo one Christmas season as I was invited to preach two conferences for the same organization. One conference was all black, the other all white, both going on at the same time, ten minutes apart from each other. I cannot even begin to articulate the sadness in my soul. My initial inclination was to throw a flag and call a penalty at what I diagnosed to be McGavran's homogenous unit principle rearing its head once again. I was angry.

God wouldn't let me bury my anger this time. His Holy Spirit began to nudge me gently, persistently. I was no longer comfortable playing Monday morning quarterback and shouting out suggestions. I had to become a part of the solution. While my connections to the African American church kept the door open to return, I knew that would not be home for me. My heart began to long for an address that was multiethnic. I didn't know how I would get there, but I let God know that when He was ready my answer would be yes.

You may be surprised to hear me say that I do not believe that every church should be multiethnic. In many of our communities, this is just impossible. I've never been to places like North Dakota, but I would imagine planting a multiethnic church there would be improbable in many of her sections. However, if your community has various ethnicities and your church is not actively taking steps toward all of them, then I think we have ventured into an area of sin. Both white flight and passive indifference to the diverse faces around our church are an affront to the eclectic gospel of Jesus Christ. Lord forgive us.

There are three wonderful truths about the multiethnic church that I want to share with you. These truths have shaped my life. I have discovered that: 1) The multiethnic church is a visible demonstration of the power of the gospel; 2) The multiethnic church is a witness to a diverse society; and 3) The multiethnic church is an instrument of healing.

THE MULTIETHNIC CHURCH IS A VISIBLE DEMONSTRATION OF THE POWER OF THE GOSPEL

As God began to prepare the soil of my heart to venture out into this kind of ministry, I began to study the book of Acts, and what I found startled me. I paid careful attention to Paul's church planting strategy, and realized that whenever Paul entered into a city to establish a new gospel outpost, he always had two questions: 1) Where is the synagogue (because he wanted to preach to the Jews); and 2) Where do the Gentiles hang out? When Paul was in Ephesus, he went to the hall of Tyrannus; in Athens he hiked up Mars Hill. To the Jew and Gentile alike, Paul preached Christ crucified, buried, and resurrected. Some Jews believed this gospel, and so did some Gentiles.

What Paul did next is instructive. Did he start a church on one side of town for the Gentiles, and another church on the opposite side of town for the Jews? This would seem to make sense given the fact that the two never really had any meaningful exchanges. But while this would have been culturally comfortable, Paul knew that the gospel demanded more. So Paul did the completely countercultural thing: he placed both ethnicities in one church and called upon them to do life with one another in meaningful ways. That's right. The *norm* in the first-century church was multiethnic. This truth floored me.

Now it made sense why Paul talked so extensively about such subjects as food. In a homogenous church, food is no big deal. Everyone's theology of ribs is aligned. But in a multiethnic church, food all of a sudden becomes a huge deal. Imagine the frustration a recent Jewish convert felt when he put his feet under his Gentile brother's table only to be served a half rack of ribs! So Paul immersed himself in the conflict and showed this gathering how to navigate the complexities of a diverse church.

What's more is that Paul's understanding of the gospel not only impacted his church planting strategies, it also created a new paradigm for how he personally did community. In very biographical terms, Paul invites us into his circle of friendships in 1 Corinthians 9:19–23, and what we see is that Paul has an eclectic community. He has Jewish friends and Gentile friends, quite the scandal in the first-century world. But his reasoning for his eclectic community is simple: he does it all for the sake of the gospel (1 Corinthians 9:23).

As these truths began to marinate in my mind, our church was launched. Memorial Day weekend, 2003 my wife of four years, our two sons, and a team of twenty-six people, mostly white, landed in Memphis, Tennessee, to launch Fellowship Memphis in the very city where Dr. King was killed. Our dreams were huge, funding low, and our people eager. What we were believing God for was so beyond us that if God didn't do it, we would surely fail. So we immediately went to work begging God to bless our efforts and forgive our mistakes.

> **BEFORE SHE heard the gospel preached, she saw the gospel lived.**

Today, by God's grace, we are a body of two thousand people, 65 percent white, and 35 percent African American. In a city where they said it could not be done, God is doing it, and all praise is due His name. Over the years what I have concluded about the multiethnic church is that it is the place where the power of the gospel is visibly demonstrated.

Some years ago I was shaking hands down front after church one Sunday when an elderly black woman came up to me. She squeezed my hand with all of her might, and with tears coming down her face, she told me that for years she had worked as a domestic in the city of Memphis, cleaning the homes of whites and taking care of their kids. She was here when Dr. King was killed. She recalled the curfews, and the early days of what they called busing (school integration). Then mustering up all of her strength and squeezing my hand harder, she said that she had prayed for a multiethnic church with a pastor like me. As she looked into my eyes, she said, "You, Son, are the answer to those prayers." I will never forget her. This sweet woman probably didn't remember a word I said that day, she was too busy looking to her left and to her right at blacks and whites worshiping and doing life with one another. Before she heard the gospel preached, she saw the gospel lived. I was reminded that day that the power of the multiethnic church is that it is a visible demonstration of the gospel.

A WITNESS TO A DIVERSE SOCIETY

There's a second reason why I believe the multiethnic church is necessary: it's a witness to our society that is becoming more and more diverse. Statistics say that by the year 2050 America, for the first time in her history, will become majority-minority. The growing Latino community, the proliferation of children born out of interracial marriages and relationships, along with a host of other reasons substantiate the upward trajectory of diversity in America. Already in places like California, we are catching glimpses of our coming reality—majority-minority. The face of America is literally changing.

What about the church? If our country is moving double time on a trajectory toward diversity, is the church keeping up? The answer, sadly, is no. Sociologists define a multiethnic church as one in which one ethnicity does not make up more than 80 percent of the gathering. This is what we would call the 80/20 rule, a very generous rule I might add. If we took this benchmark and asked how many of our worshiping communities would qualify as multiethnic, you'd be astounded by the answer. Currently there are over three hundred thousand congregations of all faiths in our country. This number includes Jews, Muslims, Buddhists, and so on. Of the three hundred thousand plus worshiping communities, only 7 ½ percent would qualify as multiethnic. Now if we were to apply the 80/20 rule to those congregations who claim to worship the resurrected Jesus, that number falls from 7 ½ percent to 2 ½ *percent.*

You may want to re-read the previous paragraphs. Our nation is rapidly becoming more and more ethnically diverse, while the church of Jesus Christ has been entrenched in homogeneity. Some may look at this as an occasion to throw their hands in the air and give up. I actually see a wonderful opportunity in front of us to change the trajectory of the church back to her first-century roots where multiethnic was the norm. I believe that the multiethnic church in twenty-first century America is a witness to a diverse society. What an opportunity we have before us!

THE MULTIETHNIC CHURCH IS
AN INSTRUMENT OF HEALING

Dr. King wrote his "Letter from a Birmingham Jail" to share his hope of seeing the playing field finally leveled. For the thirty-nine years that Dr. King lived, and the thirteen or so that he labored as the leader of the civil rights movement, he used the church to mobilize the people to force the government's hand. Any historian will tell you that his strategy worked. Yet half a century later the economic and education gaps that continue to exist force us to conclude that the playing field is still slanted away from minorities. When affirmative action tools like the NFL's Rooney Rule have to be utilized, we know that we still have yet to overcome. But why do we still have so much work to do in the aftermath of the civil rights act?

Congress cannot legislate hearts. The Senate cannot heal hurts. The Supreme Court cannot demand the restoration of relationships. Essentially, Washington, DC, cannot dress the greatest wound that continues to plague our nation: racism. But I know of a Great Physician who can cure what ails us. I know a Suffering Servant by whose stripes we are healed. There is no pain that Christ cannot heal, and God has ordained that the instrument of healing would be His bride, the church of the resurrected Savior! It is the crucified Christ who has delegated the church to be His recovery room. I am a witness to the power of the multiethnic church to heal our afflictions and wounds, specifically the wound of racism.

My friend Larry Acosta says that we hurt in isolation but heal in community. I found this to be true for me. My pathway out of darkness did not come by reading books, or even reading Scripture. It ultimately came by me allowing myself to be loved by the very ones I did not like. I know this past sentence causes some to wince, but it's true. And it's a biblical principle. When Jesus chose the twelve disciples, He knew that He was dealing with twelve men who had been culturally conditioned to look down on those who were ethnically different from them—people like the Samaritans, Canaanites, and the Gentiles in general. This was a bit of a problem because Jesus was going to call them to take the gospel to the world. So their prejudice—and dare I say racism—needed to be dealt with. But exactly what did Jesus prescribe for their racism? He didn't just say read this book, or listen to My teaching. No, Jesus knew that was not enough. What these men needed were meaningful experiences with the other. They needed to get up close and personal with the very ones they despised.

So Jesus arranged for a field trip to Samaria. He let them witness a conversation with a Canaanite woman. Jesus sent Peter to stay in the home of a man who worked with dead animals (a job no respectable Jew would take on, which means Simon is in all likelihood a Gentile). He plopped Philip down in a chariot right next to a black man in Acts chapter 8. Paul hiked up Mars Hill and was surrounded by the Greek intelligentsia of his day. And when old man racism reared its head in Peter again, God saw to it that Paul's confrontation with him would be recorded for all of human history to witness. God's means of healing racism in our hearts is through shared experiences with the very people we are prejudiced against.

This is how God is healing me. The racism in my heart was merely a symptom of my pain, a pain that I had failed to completely deal with. If it seems odd that God would use a racist man to take the gospel to a people he was severely prejudiced against, then you would have to take issue with Peter, Paul, and the rest of the disciples. God didn't just use me to build His church, but He used His church to build me.

I'm not sure how my wounds would ever have been healed without a white man by the name of McLean Wilson who joined our church and wandered into my life. He was everything that I was suspicious of. White. Old money. Memphian. But somehow, McLean and his bride ended up at my house for dinner, and immediately I felt a connection. As we were finishing up dinner, McLean told me that he was leery of moving back to Memphis. He enjoyed life in North Carolina where no one knew his pedigree. While there, McLean said that he began reading about black theology. This led him to pray an unusual prayer. "Lord," McLean prayed, "I've never really had a black friend. Would You send me a black friend?" Like the eighty-year-old black woman who came up to me after a service, McLean announced to me that evening at our dinner table that I was the answer to his prayers. There was no asking what I thought about his "proposal." McLean just informed me that we were going to be pals, and immediately he went to work.

The next thing I knew McLean had set up a hunting trip where we sat in a duck blind, in the freezing cold embracing our twelve-gauge shotguns. I tried to convince McLean that I had never hunted anything before, but he could care less. My "training" was to shoot some skeet the day before, followed by a quick tutorial on where to load the shells (if that's even what you call them). Using a clock analogy, McLean looked at me with a smile on his face and told me to shoot between ten and two, or I'd take somebody's head off. That was it. As we helped to manage God's creation that day, there were plenty of high fives and substantive conversations where we began to poke and prod into each other's lives. God was healing me.

> **MY RELATIONSHIP WITH McLean dismantled my hypothesis that to be rich, Southern, and white was to be racist. McLean led me to meet four other guys from our church (all white) and we decided to form a group . . . poking in the no-fly zones of our lives.**

Over the years McLean and I have taken road trips together, enjoyed countless lunches, and poured our hearts out in prayer with each other. We've shared incredible struggles, and have said very hard things in love to each other. My relationship with McLean dismantled my hypothesis that to be rich, Southern, and white was to be racist.

My friendship with McLean led me to meet four other men from our church (all white) and we decided to form a small group. Every Monday we gather, like C. S. Lewis' Inklings, to talk about what's going on in our lives. There is no small talk, just poking in the no-fly zones of each other's lives. Through our journey together, God has used these men to return to the work He started years ago at Lake Avenue. I've learned in real time the veracity in Larry Acosta's words: we hurt in isolation but heal in community.

Time doesn't allow me to talk about other white men God has sent into my life to love me through my pain. Men like Bobby Conway, Adam Anders, and Dennis Rainey. If it wasn't for this tribe of Jesus loving men, I fear the last chapter of my life would have been overrun with anger and bitterness.

CONCLUSION

Almost five years to the day after King wrote his "Letter from a Birmingham Jail", he died on a balcony in Memphis, Tennessee. His final season was mired in tragedy. No longer were the loudest voices in his life the hostile Southern whites, or the passive "moderates" (as he would call them), but joining the chorus were a younger generation of blacks who were growing restless with his nonviolent approach. They wanted, no, they needed to retaliate by any means necessary. Shouts of "black power" were beginning to drown out "We shall overcome." In essence, these new voices were as pained as their predecessors; they just didn't know what to do with their pain, so they harnessed it for hate.

To his grave, though, King remained hopeful, refusing to allow the pain of racism to be translated into bitterness and hate. If anyone had an excuse to give up, it would have been Dr. King. The mass of hate mail he received, the threats on his life, abuse from certain government agencies, the pleas of passive clergy, and a myriad of other reasons would've made his early exit more than understandable. Yet King continued to fight, armed solely with the weapon of love. So what kept hatred from claiming King?

Any investigation into what drove Dr. King would cause one to quickly answer that he believed in the Christian ethic of love for one's enemies. While some debate whether or not King fit traditional evangelical paradigms of orthodoxy, his biblical commitment to loving his enemies is unquestioned. This was not just something he preached, it's how he lived.

King's commitment to his theological convictions was helped by the company that he kept. Yes, we know about the fraternity of black preachers that he enjoyed camaraderie with, but also in King's tribe were a group of white men who served as ravens in the wilderness, giving him the sustenance he needed to make it through the many seasons of drought. White men like Stanley Levison, Abraham Joshua Heschel, and a host of what some have labeled "liberal" white friends of King's, not only helped to keep him focused but served as visual reminders that not every white face is hostile or passive to the cause. I believe it was this community that levied the waters of pain in King's soul, keeping them from turning into a flood of hatred.

This is why the multiethnic church is necessary. If we really believe that the church is the hope of the world, and not government, then the civil rights movement was bound to be limited in its scope, for the most it could hope for was an external transformation. Yet external change, without internal transformation, breeds hypocrisy (see the Pharisees), and will leave a nation stubbing its toe against the same brick of racism. That's where the church must rise up. When she functions on all cylinders, she becomes an unstoppable force that God uses to change hearts, and now the stage is set for even more progress.

The multiethnic church becomes even more valuable, because part of the very thing Christians seek to accomplish outside her walls (here I'm speaking in terms of horizontal reconciliation), they are experiencing in real time within her walls, and around her dinner tables. The vessels of healing are experiencing healing themselves. How can the church speak with any authenticity against racism, systemic poverty, and injustice if within her homogenous ranks are *just* the rich, or *just* blacks. But it's when the multiethnic (and I should add, the multiclass) church speaks out that now we add credibility to the very message we proclaim in the eyes of the world. If the torrential force of the first church as found in the book of Acts is to become our twenty-first-century reality, then the faces of most of our churches must look like the faces of the first-century church: multiethnic.

Dear Dr. King,

I remember my first encounter with segregation, when as a child my dad and I stopped at a local bus station for lunch. The dining areas for whites and blacks were separated. Though small and unable fully to comprehend, I knew something was wrong.

Since that time, I have read and reread your writings. As I reflect on your Birmingham jail letter, I can see its relevance for the church today.

I am the pastor of a predominately white church located in a fairly wealthy, old neighborhood in my city. Over the years it would not have been natural or intuitive for our church to create an intentional, intimate, multiethnic environment. During the time our nation was reeling from racial injustices and you were leading many of the protests against those injustices, our church reached a particularly low moment. In fact, at that point in time, we would've been one of the churches over whom you expressed your disappointment.

Over the years, against the backdrop of that low moment, our church has been listening and learning and changing in dramatic ways, and I have seen the hand of God at work, even recently, as one of our college students, deeply convicted by the monoethnicity of her college sorority, took a stand that resulted in significant change on her campus. As the leaders of my church and I have intentionally taken steps to unite with our African American brothers and sisters, we have been actively meeting the needs of our community and planting multiethnic churches.

We've come a long way from that day at the bus station. Yet my elders and I are convinced we still have a long way to go.

We're trusting God for continued grace to proclaim and faithfully exemplify the gospel of Christ, as we seek to advance His kingdom among a diverse people, committed to growing together as one family.

Thank you for the trails you blazed toward this end.

Gratefully yours,

Pastor Sandy Willson

6

WHY TRADITIONAL, SUBURBAN CHURCHES CAN'T WAIT

Sandy Willson

INDELIBLY IMPRINTED upon my mind is a memory from my childhood in the 1950s. I recall walking into the local bus station with my father to get a sandwich for lunch and noticing that there was a separate little room in the back where all the black folks ate together. Why do I remember that? Because, even as a child, it occurred to me that something is not right with the world when people are divided or excluded by the color of their skin.

I was a teenager when Martin Luther King Jr. was assassinated, but I have recently read and reread a number of Dr. King's writings and sermons, which I find to be suffused with a radiance and power that can only be described as prophetic. We know there were several influences in his life, Mohandas K. Gandhi being one of them. But, without a doubt, the dominant and controlling influence in his life was the Christian Scriptures and the life of Jesus Christ.

In his "Letter from a Birmingham Jail," he expresses frustration and disappointment with both the black church and the white church, but his critique of the white church is especially relevant to our day. The historical record of moral failure and social insensitivity by individual Christians and by the institutional church is a reality that we must face in every generation. We, of course, acknowledge a long line of brave and faithful Christians who rose to confront the evils of their age; but we must also remember that it was the church that called for the infamous Crusades and the Inquisitions. It was church people who defended slavery, Plessy v. Ferguson, and Jim Crow laws. And it was the church who refused the admittance of black Christians to their worship services in the 1950s and 60s. The lack of thoughtful engagement by the church with the injustices of our own day, although perhaps more subtle, must also be acknowledged.

In a book entitled *Divided by Faith*, written fourteen years ago by Michael Emerson and Christian Smith, the authors made it clear that, although our civil statutes have happily changed, there is, what they call, a deep "racialization" in the American culture that causes great disparity and injustice in our society. This racialization is increasingly covert, deeply imbedded in our institutions, and virtually invisible to most white people. For example:

- There are two unemployed blacks for every one unemployed white (rather constant since 1950);
- Black median income is 62% of whites (59% in 1967);
- One in three blacks lives below the poverty line vs. one in eleven whites; Median net worth of blacks is 8% of whites;
- In a nationwide study of Medicare patients, white Americans are three times as likely to receive needed coronary bypass surgery over black patients;
- African American babies die two times as often as white babies;
- Four times as many African American mothers (compared to white mothers) die in childbirth;
- Six times as many African American males are murdered as whites;
- In marriage: in America 30% of Koreans marry non-Koreans, 40% of Chinese marry non- Chinese, 50% of Japanese

marry non-Japanese, 60% of Native Americans marry non-Native Americans, 2% of African Americans marry non-African Americans.[1]

But consider Michael Emerson's thesis in *Divided by Faith*: "A strong Christian faith among whites has actually made them less effective in solving the problems of racialization because: 1) they tend to focus on individual piety rather than institutional transformation; and 2) their churches, eager to grow numerically, tend to cater to the specific felt needs of one particular homogenous sector of society rather than on calling peoples of various cultures to love and serve each other in a multicultural community."[2]

TOO OFTEN IN THE American evangelical church, we act as though the mission of planting multiethnic churches belongs solely to those who are members of such churches.

Armed with this critique, we better understand Dr. King's charge to the white church in his famous letter:

I have been so greatly disappointed with the white church and its leadership . . .

I do not say that as one of the negative critics who can always find something wrong with the church. I say it as a minister of the gospel, who loves the church; who was nurtured in its bosom; who has been sustained by its spiritual blessings and who will remain true to it as long as the cord of life shall lengthen . . .

But the judgment of God is upon the church as never

before. If the church of today does not recapture the sacrificial spirit of the early church, it will lose its authentic ring, forfeit the loyalty of millions, and be dismissed as an irrelevant social club with no meaning for the twentieth century . . .[3]

We must continue to hear Dr. King's words as we contemplate a movement of multiethnic churches in our country. Too often in the American evangelical church, we act as though the mission of planting multiethnic churches belongs solely to those who are members of such churches. We need to change both our thinking and our conduct—and also our sense of urgency.

Even a cursory examination of the New Testament reveals to the reader that God intends to bring people of all races and ethnicities into His one new society. In the first century A.D., no division among human beings was greater than that between Jew and Gentile, but Jesus very intentionally sent His apostles not only to evangelize all the nations but also to baptize them into the new society, the church of Jesus Christ. The famous "central section" of Luke's gospel account tells the story of Jesus ministering among the despised Samaritans; and upon His resurrection He repeatedly exhorts His disciples to go to all the nations.

The church, in her imperfection, has always experienced a combination of Spirit-inspired racial inclusion and fleshly motivated racial exclusion. In the early pages of Acts, we read that Philip evangelized the Samaritans and an Ethiopian eunuch, Peter evangelized Roman soldiers and their families, and early evangelists from Cypress and Cyrene preached to Hellenists in Antioch; but it is also true that many of the Christians scattered by Stephen's persecution preached only to Jews (Acts 11:19), and the early church was plagued with ethnocentric Judaizing in almost every place churches were planted. The church of every age must address decisively the big questions of racial prejudice: "why?" and "what now?"

In Memphis, Tennessee, as in many cities and towns in the southern United States, the major ethnic groups are Caucasian Americans, African Americans and, more recently, Hispanic Americans. Unlike New York, Chicago, or Boston, which are blessed with scores of vibrant ethnic communities, many Southern cities are historically "binary" in their racial demographic. As we all know, these two ethnic groups—Caucasian and African American—share a long, tortured history on this continent, and the residual levels of hurt, resentment, fear, and distrust often remain very high. When ethnic groups get along well together, their children begin to intermarry; but the low rates of intermarriage between whites and blacks clearly indicate continuing alienation and isolation from each other. This points to why multiethnic churches in the American South are so crucial to the ministry of the gospel. In the first century, some brothers from Cypress and Cyrene saw the need clearly in Antioch and did something about it. We must do it in our age, as well.

The specific question we want to address in this chapter is how historically white, suburban churches can faithfully promote multiethnic ministry. We shall see that there are things we must do, both internally and externally, in order to be faithful to the gospel.

THE INTERNAL MINISTRY

The church I pastor is an amazing assembly of God's people who faithfully and generously serve the Lord. Many times each year, I am simply stunned by their acts of kindness, by their sacrificial efforts to serve the poor in our city and to evangelize the lost around the world, and by their bold displays of Christian character. Anyone who knows me well and knows this congregation well knows that I am not worthy to untie the straps of their sandals. At the same time, we are historically a dominantly Caucasian church in a fairly wealthy, old neighborhood of our city. This cultural location has heavily influenced our outlook and our habits. Let's just put it this way: over the years, it would not have been natural or intuitive for us to create an intentional, intimate, multiethnic environment in our fellowship. Many churches in our country could tell similar stories. What should churches like ours do to lead our congregation in gospel-mandated, multiethnic ministry, especially in the South?

CAST A BIBLICAL VISION

The first thing leaders must do is to ask the Lord to give them a robust, biblical vision for how He might be pleased to change and to use our congregations in His mission. Everyone to some degree is a product of his or her environment. We have blind spots. We have prejudices. We are selfish and lazy at times. We need to repent. Even biblical Joseph needed to repent.

Joseph is one of those rare characters in the Bible, like Daniel, about whom very little bad is written in the Scriptures. (Of course, he should not have been boastful in front of his brothers, but give him a break, he was only seventeen years old.) Having been sold into slavery by his brothers, Joseph's subsequent career in Egypt is an amazing story of God's faithfulness to him and to Israel and of Joseph's trust in the Lord. But even Joseph had to learn an important lesson from God about including all of our family. We can apply this lesson in the church. You will remember that when famine came to Canaan, the sons of Jacob traveled to Egypt for supplies, not knowing, of course, that their brother Joseph was not only alive but was now also prime minister of Egypt! When they came before him to purchase food, they did not recognize him. He was in native dress and spoke the native language of Egypt, but he understood every Hebrew word they said to each other.

Through all the journeys and events of Genesis 42–44, one thing is clear: although Joseph is being remarkably kind to his brothers by not oppressing them (as they did to him) or killing them (as they contemplated doing to him), there is only one brother to whom he really wants to reveal himself and upon whom he wants to bestow his wealthy privileges: his full, younger brother Benjamin. This is understandable. His half brothers had treated him treacherously. Joseph was being extremely gracious not to retaliate against them. He planned to serve their needs with generous supplies but to keep only Benjamin in his home in Egypt.

This is just like the church. We generally want to be nice to all of our brothers. We write checks for their welfare, we want to be sure that they have food and clothing; we host occasional joint worship services; but we often have no interest in living in the same household with them. This is not just a white problem; it is a black problem, too. Professor James Cone says that the big conundrum that black theology seeks to solve is how an oppressed people can worship the same God as the God of their oppressors. Genesis 45 reveals the answer: God broke Joseph's heart by showing him that he could not have Benjamin without also having the rest of the family. Joseph sobbed so loudly that all the Egyptians heard it. I think he wept because, for the first time, he realized the grand scale of God's grace in giving him all of his family back to him as family—not just people to tolerate, or people to help, but people to love in family fellowship. Joseph's grace was not gracious enough. Man's love is not God's love; and we, the people of God, must learn to experience and express the full extent of God's love.

This is the grand gospel vision that Christian leaders must recapture in order for us to lead the gospel mission. In our particular setting in east Memphis, where 65 percent of our church members come from eight zip codes, and those eight zip codes are 30 percent African American, it only seems reasonable that we would envision those same demographics for our congregation. We must cast a vigorous gospel vision for our congregations. As we do, so often we find that God will begin to move our congregations toward the vision He has given us.

TEACH THE CONGREGATION

Any student of Paul's letters knows how often he taught on matters of multiethnicity and multiculturalism. In Galatians, Ephesians, Romans, 1 Corinthians, and Philippians, to name the most obvious examples, Paul boldly taught how we must treat each other as family. If the inclusion of all ethnic groups into the local church is as big an issue as we think it is, our churches need to hear solid biblical truth on this topic with practical advice about what to do. The practical teaching needs to include both historic and current practices of the church that violate the biblical standards so that every generation understands precisely what we mean by biblical racial justice; for without racial justice, there will be no racial inclusion.

Caucasians need to understand, for example, that because of historic racial injustices, white skin in this country is literally worth about one million dollars over a normal life span. Because of this, if white people do nothing to reverse it, they are benefiting from and collaborating with evil. Churches that do not teach these truths probably will not be able to help very much in the advancement of multiethnic ministry. But a word of warning: many who teach on this matter in dominantly Caucasian churches have found that this teaching is not always highly popular with every one of our members.

Second Presbyterian Church in Memphis is a 169-year-old church with a great history of faithful perseverance through yellow fever epidemics, economic depressions, times of war, and seasons of tumult, both nationally and locally. She has also lived through years of tremendous racial strife, including the antebellum period, the Civil War, Reconstruction, the Jim Crow era, and the civil rights revolution of the 1950s and 60s. We delight in the fact that one of our charter members in 1844 was an African American and that local oral history includes the story of an elementary school on our church's first property for the benefit of children of slaves.

Probably our lowest moment as a church, however, was in 1964–65, when our nation was reeling from racial injustices and from the many protests and struggles against them. Some local students and some folks from our local chapter of the NAACP came to our church to protest our segregationist culture and were denied entrance to our sanctuary in 1964. Eventually, by 1965, our congregation took a bold public stand to integrate the church under the able leadership of our senior minister at that time. This subsequently prompted 225 people to leave our church; but much damage had been done to our church and our reputation in the community.[4]

To this day, it is still painful for us, even as a progressive, evangelical church, to talk about these events publicly. It is embarrassing. It is frustrating. We get defensive when others make simplistic, moralistic statements about the events and the people (our relatives), especially if these comments are made by people not old enough to understand the differences between today's culture and that of the 1960s in the South. Even though I lived through that period and have served as pastor for nineteen years, I still cannot speak about our racial history without offending a few of our people.

In the spring of 2013 I was preaching through Ephesians. When I came to Ephesians 2:11–22, where Paul speaks of the new humanity being one in Christ, I asked the question: If we were to have applied this truth radically to ourselves during the protests of 1964, what should we have done? How should Christians respond when some of their family members—brothers and sisters in Christ—are unjustly denied their rights? After admitting that if I had been here, we would not have done as well as we did under our senior minister at that time, I also articulated a radical solution: the entire congregation, led by the senior minister, should have worshiped on the front lawn of the church in solidarity with the protestors who were denied entrance by our elders.

Several of our members told me they had been helped by the

sermon, but I also got serious push back from about a half dozen of our longtime members. My words hurt them and angered them. To criticize our forbearers seemed to some of them to be arrogant and unnecessarily provocative. Since I love our people so much, it hurt me too, but I explained to each one of them why it is necessary that every Christian generation assess the behaviors and words of the previous generation. It is essential that we teach the next generation how to think and act, even if it humbles us.

Here's what I didn't know at the time: one of our college students, Sims Munn, was listening online. After the sermon, she stared at her computer screen, deeply convicted by the monoethnicity of her college sorority of which she was an officer. She asked God to show her how to respond to His Word and expressed to Him her willingness to follow His lead whatever that might be. She returned in the fall to her university, the University of Alabama. During the sorority rush, several of her fellow student leaders informed her that in a private membership meeting they witnessed one of the alumni advisors of her sorority single-handedly striking the name of an African American student from the rush list. These leaders understood exactly why this advisor did this: solely because the girl rushing was African American. When Sims discovered this, she knew she must advocate for this student and could not formally associate with any organization that would deny membership to a person on the basis of ethnicity. She went to her fellow sorority officers and protested. Because some of the leadership claimed nothing could be done to remedy this specific offense, Sims packed her bags and left the sorority house.

Within days she sought to work with the sorority's national office, but this office refused to respond appropriately. In light of this she knew she must resign, and she made an appointment to see the president of the university, to whom she delivered a written statement of her complaints and her demands for racial justice. When she submitted her resignation to her sorority, she gave a speech on biblically based racial justice to the entire sorority. She explained her position to them, "As a follower of Jesus Christ, who not only refuses to discriminate along racial lines but who devoted His whole life to break down such barriers, I felt I had no choice but to stand against what happened." Present in the room that evening were several girls who would play a significant role in the coming days to raise awareness on this issue and press for change, including the editor of the student newspaper.

Weeks later, the student newspaper broke the big story that detailed similar racism plaguing other sororities as well, and this story led to significant change, even extending beyond the Greek system. These events at the University of Alabama precipitated a national discussion through CNN, NPR, and USA Today, and this press coverage cast the nation's gaze upon the university administration's response. The president of the University of Alabama dictated an extension of the pledge season during which all ethnic groups would be given equal opportunity to pledge these sororities, and this presidential action finally broke the race barrier in the university Greek system. This enabled several African Americans who wanted to pledge historically white fraternities and sororities to do so.

Though many in Alabama rejoice to see these changes, very few would have known that these changes were in part instigated by a twenty-one-year-old college student who listened carefully to biblical teaching in her church. Sims is a model of how members in traditional churches must boldly implement the radical social teachings of the Scriptures. A traditional missional church cannot export what she herself does not practice.

If we do not teach our people, they sometimes do not know how to handle the subtleties of racial injustice. In order to advance multi-ethnic ministry, we have to start teaching right where we are.

UNITE THE LEADERSHIP

In order for a church to be truly multiethnic in ministry and mission, the leadership of the church must be united. This is not always easy. The apostle Paul had to confront and correct publicly even the apostle Peter on one occasion (Galatians 2:11–14)! In 2000 our elders appointed a study committee to research this topic and to propose both a policy statement and also some recommended action steps that would align us with biblical teaching on racial justice. After a year of study, they returned their report and our elders adopted an uncompromising statement on race relations at Second Presbyterian Church with a commitment to teach and model biblical justice, to hire African Americans at all levels of our staff, to use more minority vendors, to promote the development of African American owned businesses in Memphis, and to plant multiethnic churches.[5]

Over the past years, by God's grace, our leaders have been united in intentionally calling African American pastors and other ministry people to our staff. We have, with our partners, initiated leadership development programs and academic programs for African American adults in the community. We have actively participated in the Mid-South Minority Business Council. We have ordained African American officers and led hundreds of African American students to Christ. We have increased our African American membership, and have planted two multiethnic churches in Memphis. And our elders believe we still have a very long way to go.

If folks feel that this kind of "affirmative action" equals "reverse discrimination," we can gently lead them to the apostolic solution to the racial controversy in Acts 6:1–7, where the men appointed to resolve a serious ethnic crisis all appear to be from the minority Hellenistic population! It's called Christian wisdom.

Within our churches we must endeavor to cast a biblically based vision, faithfully teach in season and out of season, and unite our leaders around a plan of action.

THE EXTERNAL MINISTRY

Listen and Learn

When I came to our church nineteen years ago, one of the first things I did was join a racial reconciliation seminar led by one of our fine elders, Frank Jemison, and by an African American leader in town, Steve Allison. Over many weeks we were taught the history of race relations in our part of the country, the continuing racism in our culture, and the ways to develop better mutual understanding. Wisely, we were paired with another participant of the opposite race to meet regularly to discuss these topics. My partner was Rev. Dr. Jerry Ivery. He gave me a great education on race relations in Memphis, for which I shall always be grateful. Caucasians, like me, usually know a whole lot less than we think we know.

Second Presbyterian also works with sixty ministry agencies in Memphis. They are all our teachers. We have learned from outstanding leaders like Larry Lloyd and Howard Eddings of the *Memphis Leadership Foundation*, from JoeAnn Ballard and Ephie Johnson at the *Neighborhood Christian Centers*, from Ken Bennett at *Streets Ministries*, from Tony Wade at *Repairing the Breach Ministries*, from Steve Nash at *Advance Memphis*, from Gib Vestal at *Memphis Athletic Ministries*, and from many, many more. We ask questions, we listen to them teach, we study their methods, we search for ways to partner, and, in the process, we begin to learn about what a city and a neighborhood need.

Engage

Years ago, I asked Dr. David Anderson, pastor of Bridgeway Community Church in Columbia, Maryland, what he would suggest we do at Second Presbyterian to promote multiethnic ministry. In his unique way, he told me a little story: If one owns an orange grove but wants to mix in grapefruits, he should continue to cultivate his existing orange grove and add a new grove consisting of both oranges and grapefruits; that is, we must innovate as much as possible within our own congregation, but we must especially innovate beyond the existing structures of Second Presbyterian Church.

Sometime later I went to see Dr. Carol Johnson, superintendent of Memphis City Schools, to ask if there were any new ways Second Presbyterian Church could help the cause of public education in our city. I told her why I was there and then hesitatingly—almost apologetically—stated that perhaps she wouldn't want to use our people since so many of us patronized the local private schools; we thought our future involvement might end up being an embarrassment to her and to her staff.

She just looked at me quizzically and asked, "Rev. Willson, do your people love children?"

"Yes, ma'am," I said.

"You'll do just fine," she continued, "let me hand you over to my deputy who is in charge of our community partnerships, and you and she can develop a plan for us."

We eventually adopted Berclair Elementary School, 90 percent of whose students are on the government free lunch program. Three hundred of our members picked up glass from the school playground, planted grass for a front lawn, cooked barbecue for the parents' meetings (attendance quadrupled), painted classrooms, and read to students, 40 percent of whom were Hispanic. Our Sunday school classes each adopted a Berclair classroom for prayer and ministry. The school had been seriously considered for closure for its poor performance, but over the years, the standardized test scores began to rise. When local principals called Berclair principal, Dr. Sam Shaw, to ask how the transformation happened, he told them "I'm not really sure, but I think it has something to do with Jesus."

Following our efforts in the school, we began ESL classes, after-school Bible studies, and a soccer team, eventually leading to the incorporation of a Community Development Corporation. We later planted Esperanza Church in the Berclair community. We all learned something very important: the gospel of cross-cultural love really works.

Be the Church—Plant Churches

The question still remains as to how a traditional, still dominantly Caucasian, largely professional church can advance multiethnic church planting and underresourced church planting. The answer begins with a candid, biblically based assessment of our community's needs. Here's our bottom line conclusion: Memphis needs Shalom, the peace of God; and in order for Memphis to have Shalom, her 127 neighborhoods have to have shalom; and in order for each of those neighborhoods to have shalom, those neighborhoods must have their basic human needs met; and in order that their basic needs be met, every neighborhood must have healthy, holistic, Bible-believing, gospel-centered, neighborhood-based local churches. This is where resource churches, like ours, come in.

> **IF YOU BELONG to a monocultural church, you are probably not qualified on your own to plant or lead a multiethnic church plant; therefore, you must partner with those fellow evangelicals who know what they are doing or who will take the time to learn.**

Who should lead the effort to plant and revitalize neighborhood churches? Parachurch organizations? Charitable foundations?

Seminaries? No, the church must plant the church! This is our mandate. The church in Antioch sent out Paul and Barnabas to evangelize and establish churches, which is exactly what they did. We must, too. In our day, of course, we are splintered into thousands of denominations; therefore, we must make the effort to reconnect with our brothers and sisters in evangelical churches to take responsibility jointly in the spiritual welfare of our city and to plan together as we revitalize and plant churches in our neighborhoods.

If you belong to a monocultural church, you are probably not qualified on your own to plant or lead a multiethnic church plant; therefore, you must partner with those fellow evangelicals who know what they are doing or who will take the time to learn. Sometimes, we simply need to support the work of others in our community, even when it costs us members and money.

When Bryan Loritts came to town and shared with us what he felt God had put upon his heart to do in Memphis, we recognized immediately God's answer to our prayers. God was sending us a man who had a heart for multiethnic church planting, who was theologically and spiritually sound, and who was blessed with tremendous leadership gifts. Fellowship Church in Memphis has set a new standard in our city for how to plant healthy, growing multiethnic churches. It is our honor to support and collaborate with him. But Bryan's wasn't the first one nor the most recent one. Others have labored very effectively for years, without much public notice, steadily teaching, leading, and nurturing a few small multiethnic churches, with all of their challenges. They are all worthy of our prayers, our encouragement, and our emulation of their commitment to racial reconciliation. They need to hear regularly from traditional church leaders how important their ministry is to our city.

At other times, we need to take initiative, either as "mother churches" or as a collaborative group of churches to plant new churches or to revitalize the old ones for all of our communities. At Second Presbyterian, virtually all of our major church planting efforts are either in under-resourced neighborhoods or in neighborhoods intentionally chosen for a multiethnic work. We believe that the suburbs, generally speaking, have plenty of human and financial resources to provide for new church plants; therefore, we now focus our resources on the places of greatest urgency and least resources. On occasion we do lend financial support for Memphis suburban churches, like St. Patrick Presbyterian, planted and pastored by Jim Holland or like the Harvest Church planted and pastored by Kennon Vaughn, because we are convinced that churches like these will soon join in the effort to spend considerable effort and resources for the underserved neighborhoods of our city.

When we seek to plant multiethnic churches, we look at the neighborhoods that seem to be most suitable demographically and most needy of such a church. Second Presbyterian planted All Saints Church in Midtown Memphis, pastored by Waring Porter and David Stenberg. It is a beautiful mosaic of white and black, professional and poor. Downtown Presbyterian, planted by Second under the leadership of Richard Rieves and Chris Davis, is about 35 percent African American and about 55 percent Caucasian and is also reaching a very diverse group of people. The younger church planters from all denominations now coming to our city are most often praying for God to give them an effective multiethnic ministry. For this we are very grateful.

These efforts require prayer and people and money and time. Established churches have an important role to play. We must freely send our members into these works. We must help new church planters connect with leaders in our city, and we must resource them with finances, information, training, and prayer. We then must join with them to strategize and collaborate in planting or revitalizing other churches.

As a giddy grandfather, I can report great joy in observing and participating in my children's and grandchildren's growth in the Lord. Established churches and their leaders, just like doting grandfathers, must aid and abet those who plant gospel-centered, multiethnic churches; and then, of course, just as with our children, these new churches become our greatest teachers.

With the tremendous need for multiethnic churches in this country, those of us pastoring dominantly monoethnic churches can no longer wait. The day has come, the men and women leaders are being raised up, the opportunities are vast, and our resources must be fully deployed to this urgent task.

In January of 1957, one hundred black clergymen met at Ebenezer Baptist Church in Atlanta to form the Southern Christian Leadership Conference. Shortly after he was elected its first president, Dr. King published an article explaining his philosophy of nonviolent resistance and his deepest convictions concerning the ultimate victory of biblical justice.

> [We know] that in [our] struggle for justice [we have] cosmic companionship. This belief that God is on the side of truth and justice comes down to us from the long tradition of our Christian faith. There is something at the very center of our faith which reminds us that Good Friday may reign for a day, but ultimately it must give way to the triumphant beat of the Easter drums. Evil may so shape events that Caesar will occupy a palace and Christ a cross, but one day that same Christ will rise up and split history into A.D. and B.C., so that even the life of Caesar must be dated by his name. So in Montgomery we can walk and never get weary, because we know that there will be a great camp meeting in the promised land of freedom and justice.[6]

Dear Dr. King,

My relationship with your legacy stretches back as far as I can remember. I still remember images, from my childhood, of "strange fruit hanging from poplar trees" and dogs biting at the feet of those who look like me still torment my sense of righteousness and justice. Today I am still haunted by the brutality and hatred of the aggressors.

As I read your letter and, more specifically, your comments about the early church—"it was not merely a thermometer that recorded the ideas and principles of popular opinion; it was a thermostat that transformed the mores of society"—and early Christians—the Christians pressed on, in the conviction that they were 'a colony of heaven' called to obey God rather than man"—I think of today's church. We have come a long way, but I fear that if we are not careful, some may run the risk of becoming like those critical clergymen of your day, avoiding rocking the boat and remaining silent.

As we consider the continued legacy of Christ through your sacrifices, it's clear the gospel requires us to live differently. I'm glad to say many Christian leaders from diverse backgrounds realize we cannot make the mistake of being indifferent or silent on any points restricting the fulfillment of God's kingdom plan. In light of this there are greater efforts, by the grace of God, to see Christians from diverse backgrounds doing life and pursuing the cause of Christ together.

You said the 11 a.m. hour is the most segregated hour of the week. In many ways that's still true. My dream is that, in dealing with injustice and indifference, we will mend the tear that rips through the soul of the church at this hour each week and become the most diverse reflection of God's glory on earth, all because we decided to "obey God rather than man."

Gratefully yours,

Pastor Albert Tate

7

THE MULTICULTURAL CHURCH BEGINS IN YOUR LIVING ROOM

Albert Tate

I GREW UP A YOUNG black boy in the rural town of Pearl, Mississippi. Both of my parents were students at Tougaloo College and recall watching the Woolworth sit-ins in Jackson, Mississippi. I remember the names and stories of those daring enough to rebel in peaceful determination against the oppressive powers that be. Images of "strange fruit hanging from poplar trees" and dogs biting at the feet of those who look like me still torment my sense of righteousness and justice.

I am haunted by the brutality and hatred of the aggressors, but at the same time I am inspired by the courage and the faithfulness of my brothers and sisters who fought in those moments. Their courage has shaped me in ways that I could not even begin to imagine. It has shaped how I see life. It has shaped my culture. It has shaped me. The tragic reality of our day is that this legacy has been relegated to history books and museums, and is rarely acknowledged with more than a passive remembrance and academic recognition. Whenever I watch the historic films and see the news clips, I am struck by the fact that the fallen heroes and heroines look like me. I am a part of that story. I cannot help but develop a familial sense of indebtedness to their legacy. There is a voice inside of me, very natural and human, that continually reminds me, *"Someone has died, and that ought to change the way I live . . ."*

During my time at Fuller Seminary, I had the privilege of taking a black theology class with Dr. Ralph Watkins. One of our assignments was to watch the miniseries *Roots* in its entirety. This multi-night TV movie was a television event in 1977 that traced the plight of blacks from colonial times through the aftermath of the American Civil War. I remember watching it as a kid in the 80s. Watching this encore showing was an awestriking reminder of the enormous sacrifice that was required for me to use the restroom without first checking to see whether it said "whites" or "coloreds" above the door. People gave their lives so that I might sip water from a fountain without having to make sure it was for "coloreds only." This experience compounded my sense of indebtedness, as I could not help but be overwhelmed by the high price that was paid for my freedom. O, the debt that I owe!

THE KING OF KINGS

As Christians, our indebtedness becomes broader than the pursuit of social justice; it is part of a much larger story. The sacrifice of our Lord and Savior, Jesus Christ, permanently alters our relationships with those who have gone before us. The hope of the civil rights movement must be more than the simple matching of names with dates and the memorization of speeches in school. We are called to recognize that the dream Dr. King proclaimed from the steps of the Lincoln Memorial was inherited from a King and Savior who not only sacrificed to come to earth in human likeness, but ultimately sacrificed His very life in pursuit of reconciliation. The stage was set two thousand years in advance for Dr. King's reconciliatory quest. This truth inextricably links the past, present, and future in our pursuit of freedom. We cry out to God, "Thy Kingdom come, Thy will be done!"

It is not enough to fight, however passionately, for an arbitrary and cultural idea of freedom today, if that fight is not in pursuit of God's kingdom coming to earth. As Christians we are emboldened by the legacy of Dr. King and of the men and women who fought bravely toward the fulfillment of the reconciliatory quest of the gospel, toward the ultimate goal of perpetuating the legacy of Jesus Christ Himself, the ultimate hero of reconciliation.

We are promised that one day the Lord will reconcile all things and all people to Himself, and I am convinced that this hope for the future must change the way we live in the present. Revelation 7:9 reveals to us that every nation, tribe, people, and tongue will gather before the throne of Christ and proclaim him King and Ruler. There will be no segregation in this heavenly throng. There will be no white section, black section, Asian section, or Latino section (although we know if there *were* a black section, the music would be off the chain). Instead, there will be one holy and united people gathered for one singular purpose: to glorify the Almighty One. Gentiles and Jews, blacks and whites, former rivals in the world, will come together in response to Jesus and His unifying sacrifice.

GOING THROUGH SAMARIA

It may come as no surprise to you that Jesus spent a lot of His time in places that were deemed culturally inappropriate. He confused people left and right with his unrelenting affection for those He seemingly had no business being in relationship with. Jesus' approach to the Samaritans was no exception.

The Samaritans and the Jews had a standing grievance against one another. More accurately, their grievances were so many and so long-standing that their cultures had spent generations avoiding each other. Centuries prior to Jesus' time, the Samaritans had been a Jewish culture during their exile from Jerusalem. When that exile was lifted, the Samaritans had the opportunity to return to Jewish territory, but elected to stay in Samaria, where they had the freedom to intermarry with other nations and entertain foreign gods. Needless to say, the Jews and Samaritans soon became experts at segregation, which conveniently allowed the two peoples to go lifetimes without any interaction. This served only to intensify the legacy of loathing in their hearts for one another. And yet, we see Jesus taking every opportunity in the Gospels to bridge the gap between them.

WE WILL SOON find ourselves in the trap the disciples are caught in as they begin to walk around Samaria out of habit, only to notice that Jesus is going a different way.

In John 4 Jesus and His disciples are making their way from Judea back toward Galilee, when they come to a crossroads. To go one way would take them on the road most frequently traveled by the Jewish people. This road was much longer, but provided the convenience of avoiding Samaria entirely. The other road went directly through enemy territory. Although the road *through* Samaria was significantly shorter, the cultural tensions between the Jews and the Samaritans were so high that the road all the way around was more appealing.

But Jesus takes the second option: the way that was shorter when measured by the required number of steps, but much longer when measured by the requirements of the traveler's heart. Not only did Jesus opt to go through Samaria, but John 4:4 tells us that Jesus "*had to*" go through Samaria. His mission gave Him no choice but to face the tension head-on, and a miraculous interaction ensues between Jesus and the Samaritan woman at the well.

The mission of the church, the pursuit of the legacy of Christ, cannot simply be about business and culture as usual. If we allow it to be so simple, we will soon find ourselves in the trap the disciples are caught in as they begin to walk around Samaria out of habit, only to notice that Jesus is going a different way. How often this conflict arises when we attempt to follow Jesus! We set out with the best of intentions, and soon find ourselves not following Him but expecting Him to follow us. The sin in us longs to travel only the road that offers comfort and familiarity. Yet Jesus unapologetically walks the more challenging road, inviting us to witness what He will do if we choose to follow.

When we allow Jesus to free us from the trappings of comfort and normalcy, there are kingdom opportunities that await us. So we march into those uncomfortable places. We press forward into the vulnerable spaces that our culture has deemed inappropriate, following the example of our King who calls us to break down the barriers of race and class, to engage in kingdom work. There is no middle ground. We cannot witness the miracle of being moved by Christ if we refuse to be moved. We cannot fulfill our kingdom purpose when we are consumed with the desire to be relaxed. We cannot call Jesus "Rabbi, Teacher" if we refuse to be taught. So we cling tightly to the One who calls us to follow, trusting Him to deliver us from the affliction of complacency in exchange for the gospel message of reconciliation.

THE SILENCE THAT SCREAMED "CHANGE"

As I consider what those uncomfortable and inappropriate places look like in our context, I am reminded of my time in Bible college. I will never forget an assignment we had in my methods of evangelism class. The assignment sent us out to our local churches to evaluate their evangelistic models. Upon completing the assignment, I remember a Caucasian student whose church had adopted the "Evangelism Explosion" model. The method behind this particular model was to go door-to-door, and after greeting the person who answered, we were to pose the question, "If you were to die tonight, would you go to heaven or to hell?"

As he presented his church's approach, he shared stories of how the conversations that resulted from this method of evangelism allowed the church members to be great witnesses in their neighborhood. But then he said something very interesting, "When we would come to an African American person's home, we wouldn't offer them the gospel; we wouldn't even ask them the question. We would extend to them the business card of the local African American pastor and invite them to contact him for church."

As a young African American sitting in that class, I was irate. I became jittery with anticipation as I waited to respond; I could not wait for him to sit down so I could raise my hand and ask, "Why in the world would you not share the gospel with someone just because they did not look like you?" But as he concluded his presentation and I was ready to raise my hand, I paused and thought: *Let me not be the first person to bring the critique. It is easy for me as the black man to be offended. Let me wait and give my other classmates or my professor the opportunity to make this necessary cultural correction.* As I sat back and waited for someone else to speak up, I was amazed by the deafening silence in the room. In the silence that followed, what struck me as a gross segregationist approach ignited deep anger and frustration within me. Ultimately he would receive commendation from both the class and the professor affirming that his project and his church's evangelistic methods were admirable.

At that moment I realized that the gospel I grew up with was not the gospel we celebrated in that room. Although we sang the same worship songs in chapel and read the same Bible, we lived out this hope drastically different. I knew in that moment that my friends would leave that classroom to lead homogeneous churches, and would be fully satisfied with that. And I knew in that moment that it was absolutely unacceptable for me to perpetuate that cycle. Something happened to me that day in the classroom. My professor's silence screamed at me. I believe it was in that moment that the vision and the passion for the multiethnic church began to stir in my heart.

ELEVEN O'CLOCK AM VS. SIX O'CLOCK PM

Dr. King's diagnosis that the eleven o'clock hour is the most segregated hour of the week is tragic but true. If we are serious about the hope we have for reconciliation in Christ, the opposite ought to be true: that Sunday mornings become the most diverse reflection of God's glory on earth, not the least. Let's consider how we can work together toward the fulfillment of the Revelation prophecy: a victory that every nation, tribe, people, and tongue can get excited about.

The reality is that racial reconciliation has little to do with the programmatic, stylistic, or liturgical nuances we use to make the eleven o'clock service hour on Sunday morning more broadly appealing. It has little to do with advertising, branding, and the language we put on our church newsletters. Many a church has utilized its token minority person or its token white person in its advertising campaigns in an effort to reveal itself to the surrounding community as a place where all are welcome. While all these things matter, I would argue that we will never capture a truly diverse picture of God's kingdom at the eleven o'clock hour on Sunday morning, unless we win the six o'clock hour on Saturday night.

No, I am not talking about the six o'clock service you start on Saturday night to try out new things that gives the pastor a "dress rehearsal" for his sermon. I am talking about your living room; the place where you do life and invite people into the fold of your family. The bottom line is that our churches will never look differently if we allow our homes to remain unchanged. Is your living room monochromatic? I am not talking about your decor but rather about the people who routinely gather around your coffee table. Then take notice of how consistently the people you end up with at church look just like the people you spend your Saturday evenings with.

I am not suggesting that you forsake your current social relationships in an effort to exploit your dinner table as a ministerial device to reach a more diverse demographic! But our goal cannot simply be that we want to see more color in our sanctuary on Sunday. Laypeople and pastors alike are convicted by the monochromatic reality of their congregations on Sunday mornings. However, they are too often paralyzed by the complexities of a diverse community to make changes that would threaten the comfort of the regulars. So we relegate our efforts to Sunday morning's stage or staffing where we are safe, and maintain the expectation of familiarity in our own living rooms. Our sights need to be set on the Saturday night hour as the time when we fundamentally change the roster of people we do life with. At best, the world will look on and turn a puzzled head to the side. At worst, the world will insist that oil and water have no business mixing in the same bowl. But for better or worse, that is our call as followers of a radical and reconciliatory Savior.

Jesus was the perfect example of this. We see Him time and time again in the Gospels sharing meals, embracing, and interacting with people whom the leaders thought He had no business with. Every rule book in His time insisted that He remain clean by keeping a safe distance from the sick, the Samaritans, women, and children. What a weak message the gospel would be if Jesus had played by all the rules, kept within all the cultural bounds, and avoided seeming inappropriate at every turn. It would hardly be a story worth telling. But He broke boundaries left and right, revealing the truth of God's refusal to allow our hatred and prejudice to keep us separated.

We are called to live likewise. We are called to break through these barriers, inviting people to share life with us who do not look like us, talk like us, think like us, or even vote like us. If we target our living rooms as the primary places that are in need of the transforming power of Christ, we will inevitably see our sanctuaries transformed.

TOKENISM VS. KINGDOM VALUE

One of the questions that inevitably come up when we discuss the issue of multiculturalism in the local church is the question of *tokenism*. Do I just go find the nearest black friend and invite them over for dinner? Do I look for the closest Asian person and say, "Hey, come to my living room and then come to my church?" Is this an authentic strategy in the quest for diversity and multiculturalism? This question bears the same weight of controversy as that of Affirmative Action. At some point we need to ask the question of whether or not the kingdom of God requires "tokens."

About nine years ago my wife and I moved from Jackson, Mississippi, to Pasadena, California. I had been shepherding a small, rural, African American congregation in Jackson for about five years and had the opportunity to attend Fuller Seminary. In tandem with my acceptance to Fuller came a job offer to serve at a predominantly upper-middle class church nearby called Lake Avenue Congregational Church. At that time, Lake Avenue was a Caucasian congregation in a neighborhood whose demographics were rapidly changing. They were making their best efforts to create a culture inside the church that would mirror the culture that existed outside its walls. In order to do this, they began by taking a look around the table at their staff meetings. It did not take long to realize that they would have an impossible time connecting with the needs, longings, histories, and cultures surrounding the church with only the skills and ideas gathered around the table. They had limited context, relationships, and connections that would offer an easy touch point into the surrounding culture, so they were faced with a decision. They could keep doing business as usual and give up trying to relate, or they could intentionally pursue diversity within their staff in pursuit of a deeper connection with their surroundings.

As they dreamed about how to reach the changing demographic in their community, they decided to call me to serve on their team. Now the question is, was I a token black hire? Was I being hired to pastor the black kids or all the kids? Was I being tasked with addressing minority concerns in the church, or the concerns of the church at large? Would I be pastoring all the parents of the kids in the youth group, or did they want me just to help "put out fires" with the black parents? Ultimately my task was to be the youth pastor for *all* the kids, parents, and the church at large. That was made crystal clear in their invitation to join the team. This reflected their desire to pursue diversity through the kingdom value of honoring those people who are different from us, rather than simple tokenism.

Tokenism is the idea of indiscriminately grabbing the most convenient person of a particular demographic in order to have that color or culture represented in one's midst. An all-male board of directors might plant a token woman in their midst to give the appearance of balance; or an otherwise all-white movie cast may request the addition of a brother in order to appease the NAACP. This type of tokenism is often frowned upon or dismissed because it is a feeble attempt at appeasing a broader audience without doing the work of investing and engaging in a culture that is different from the mainstream.

What distinguishes tokenism as the world defines it from the strategic hiring of a minority individual in a church context is the recognition that our skin color, culture, language, history, and background all have value and lasting influence in God's economy. By hiring me on staff at Lake Avenue Church, the leadership recognized that my status in society held value beyond my credentials on paper. Was I qualified for the position? Did I have the education, training, and experience to fulfill the job? Yes. But I also carried a currency that is not recognized by organizations that do not seek the full reflection of God's magnificent nature. The invitation extended to me to join the organization was not a token hire because it was not a cavalier or convenient choice. But my blackness and my cultural background offered kingdom value to the staff and to the surrounding community that had previously been lacking. Lake Avenue made the decision to exchange the currency of business as usual for the kingdom currency that would assist the church in pursuing the vision of Revelation 7, and we saw amazing fruit during this season of ministry as a result.

As leaders of the church, we are called to live by a different standard, to trade and operate with a different currency. The church is the only organization in the world that recognizes the intrinsic value of every individual and people group based on their intentional creation by the Creator of all people. Each of us reflects a piece of who God is, and no two of us are exactly alike. Does it not follow logically, then, that in order to grow into a deeper knowledge of who God is, we must surround ourselves with people who are as different from us as possible? The world's economy values conformity, classified categories, and comfort. As church leaders we are called to the kingdom values of humility, reconciliation, and diversity.

GOD'S UNEXPECTED FAMILY

During my time at Lake Avenue Church, the congregation inducted Dr. Greg Waybright as the new head pastor. He extended an invitation to partner in the pulpit with him, and as we met on Tuesdays to discuss Scripture and sermon material, he quickly became a mentor and spiritual father figure for me. This relationship was extremely life giving, as he encouraged me to live into the fullness of the unique man and preacher God was raising me up to be.

I will never forget the sermon series entitled "God's Unexpected Family" where we sought to express how God brings different people together for His kingdom cause. Based largely out of the book of Ephesians, we highlighted how beautiful it is to be a part of this unexpected family of God. Being a visual preacher, I envisioned a beautiful dining room table with God's Unexpected Family gathered around it.

So that Sunday morning we set up a dining room table on the center of the stage in the sanctuary. As I preached I introduced all the different people who would be gathered around that table: the varieties of language, social class, immigration status, political affiliation, etc.

WHAT HAPPENS when you gather at a table with illegal immigrants who are your brothers and sisters in Christ?

Then I began to point out some of the tensions that would arise from the vast differences these people embodied. What happens when you gather at a table with illegal immigrants who are your brothers and sisters in Christ? What happens when you gather with someone who is suffering from a preexisting condition and cannot afford health insurance? I drew attention to political parties that Sunday, insisting that we would no longer carry the party line of Republican or Democrat but that we would instead bring with us the party line of the kingdom of God. It shapes all that we are and it shapes the table around which His family is gathered.

After preaching that Sunday, I received more hate mail than I had during the rest of my preaching career. People were infuriated by the suggestion that they should entertain illegal immigrants in any shape, form, or fashion. They were infuriated by the rising cost of health care for some, and the suggestion that they try to understand the plight of someone without health care. People defended their allegiance to politically inspired news media. They sent letters defending their political and social perspectives on every issue I had mentioned that day.

I struggled deeply with the nature of the criticism, crying out to God, "Did I not speak what You told me to speak? Did I not declare the truth of Your Scriptures?" I knew what I had preached was the truth, but that I had also brought up some very divisive questions as to how we wrestle with that truth. My intent through the sermon was to point out that issues get messy when we sit at the table together; tensions become high and we are challenged to change. The point was not to create anger but to create an awareness that life necessarily becomes messy when we sit at the table with people who do not look like us, think like us, or vote like us. In the aftermath of that Sunday, I had an honest moment with God and my family as I wondered if this would be the end of my time at Lake Avenue Church.

Later that week I got a call to come to Dr. Waybright's office. If I had received mail, I could only imagine that he must have received even more! I knew going into this meeting that if Dr. Waybright asked me to apologize or retract what I said, it would be a very difficult prospect. To my amazement, I sat down at the table and Dr. Waybright told me he had listened to the sermon and that he agreed with and supported everything I had said. He suggested he might have said it differently, but one could attribute that to my being a young African American man and his being a late fifties white male; our manners of speech would naturally be different.

Although I knew I had Dr. Waybright's private support, Sunday was still coming; and he would have to enter the pulpit and address the congregational response from the previous Sunday. Would he make an apology on my behalf? Would he go out of his way to lull the congregation back into a state of comfort?

Sunday morning came, and I snuck into the balcony, trying to avoid the authors of some of the emails I had received. I heard Dr. Waybright preach the same sermon I had preached the week before. He brought back the dining room table, and in his late fifties, Caucasian-male way he preached God's Unexpected Family. On a personal level, the affirmation of what I had preached and the risk I had taken the previous Sunday was deeply moving. On a prophetic level, I celebrated in my heart the truth of the Word of God being affirmed from the pulpit that morning.

Most importantly on a reconciliatory level was the fact that this was a white man who, in a time of controversy, stood beside me and was not silent. He spoke on my behalf. He pleaded my case. He gave me dignity and respect in a way that was unlike any I had ever received before. I felt the affirmation that was lacking in my evangelism class at Bible college all those years before. In that moment the gospel of reconciliation became something that broke down barriers and united me with this white brother along a common mission: to gather and celebrate the diverse, unexpected, and beautiful family of God.

I am so thankful for God placing Dr. Greg Waybright in my life. He chose not to remain silent. He spoke up. I can only imagine how thankful Dr. King was for the white men whom we see standing beside him in those marches, the white men we see standing behind him as he delivers the "I Have a Dream" speech, and the white pastors who did not keep silent but who fought alongside him. I am thankful for the white pastor who did not keep silent but who stood alongside me.

SOUL FOOD

When Jesus finished his conversation with the Samaritan woman at the well in John 4, he rejoined the disciples and, as one might predict, they had questions for him. However, they refused to ask what was on their minds, instead saying, "Rabbi, have something to eat." Often when Jesus is referred to as Rabbi, or "teacher," it is almost as if He takes it upon Himself to drop some unexpected knowledge in response. True to form, Jesus responded by saying, "I have food to eat that you do not know about." In saying this, Jesus revealed that the crosscultural, challenging, uncomfortable, and inappropriate interaction He had in Samaria had filled Him up with supernatural nourishment that far surpassed the nutritional value of the food the disciples were offering. The ability to satisfy one's soul comes only from the reckless pursuit of a Savior whose love knows no cultural bounds. This is the true meaning of Soul Food—it gives life where there was barrenness and isolation.

What would it look like to pursue this Soul Food for our families, for our churches? What would it look like if we gave up the pursuit of comfort and sameness in exchange for an opportunity to witness the miraculous reconciliation that occurs only when we follow the example of Christ? Are we doing life only with people who look like us, talk like us, think like us, and vote like us? Or are we willing to walk through Samaria as we journey with Christ? If we are truly following Him, we cannot help but be led down paths of reconciliation, for that is the vision for which He died. This was the vision that set the stage for Dr. King and so many others who would fight for this kingdom way of living.

We eagerly anticipate the day when the reality of Revelation 7:9 will be fully ours. Until then, we have a task before us: to cultivate kingdom communities in our midst. This begins not with Sunday morning programming but rather with your Saturday evening social calendar.

MY LIVING ROOM

Let us not forget that the transformation of our churches begins in our living rooms. In the same way in which we value and seek diversity around the staff table, we must also recognize the unequivocal importance of diversity around the dinner table. You cannot expect a change to take shape on Sunday morning that has not begun in your home. The enemy tempts us to surround ourselves with people who are just like us. "Power in numbers!" The world celebrates the majority, and seeks to magnify it even more. But we will never be changed if we do not surround ourselves with people who will challenge and nudge us from our places of comfort.

Look at your social calendar over the past six months. If you are a Republican, how many people have sat at your dinner table that voted for a Democrat in the most recent election, or vice versa? If you are an African American, how many people have you invited to dinner who have to put on a lot more sunscreen when they go to the beach? This should be a telling experience, as you examine the reality of your social calendar. In response to this revelation, ask yourself how you might look forward and make the next six months look different. Be careful not simply to look for tokens but to seek out kingdom value in the diversity of the people you surround yourself with. It is certainly not the easy way to live. In fact, it is much easier to build churches, to foster living rooms that look like what you see when you look in the mirror. But I guarantee that this kingdom way of living will permanently alter not only the nature of your six o'clock dinner on Saturday night but also the nature of the eleven o'clock service the next morning.

My wife, LaRosa, and I planted Fellowship Monrovia over two years ago. Long before the church was planted, we were part of a small group, with whom we continue to meet on a regular basis. It is a group of people that reflects the diversity of the kingdom of God whenever it gathers together: Jaki and Seth, a beautiful Asian woman and her Caucasian husband; Myra and Chris, a powerful, Latina woman of God and her African American husband; Melissa and David, a gifted and faithful Caucasian woman from Southern California and a black man from the United Kingdom; and the love of my life and I, who are both African American. On any given Wednesday, you will find us seated around the dinner table discussing life, challenges, marriage, children, and doing life together. And on any given Sunday, you will find us worshiping at Fellowship with hands lifted, glorifying God together. But that diversity on Sunday is but an extension of what we see every Wednesday night when we gather together for small group.

I pray for you, for your families, for your lives, and ultimately for your congregations, that you would experience real Soul Food. But in order for you to experience the food that truly satisfies, you will have to change the aisles that you shop in. Cross-cultural experience and reconciliation is food for your soul. When we engage with it, we honor the legacy of those who gave their lives for our personal freedom; and ultimately we honor the life and sacrifice of our Lord and Savior Jesus Christ who purchased our eternal freedom. Jesus paid it all, all to Him I owe. So I honor God with how I live, and whom I do life with.

"Guess who's coming to church?" Ultimately the answer lies in how you respond to this question, "Guess who's coming to dinner?"

Dear Dr. King,

At ten years of age I began committing portions of your letter to memory as a part of my school assignment. I spent hours practicing in anticipation of the time when I would recite what I'd memorized at my eighth-grade graduation. Little did I know that in those moments of practicing and thereafter, the impact of your words would propel me forward towards the ministry in which I am involved.

As I consider your work and where we are today, I believe our problem is not so much the white moderate as much as it is the Christian moderate of any race. Over fifty years later the church is still slow to commit to the hard work of racial harmony. This problem rests on the shoulders of Christian leadership and those who believe the imperatives of unity, harmony, and diversity seem better suited for the socially conscious rather than their fellowship. This problem rests on the shoulders of those who believe this part of the gospel is optional.

Every Sunday I have the privilege as the senior pastor of Chicago's historic Progressive Baptist Church to preach from the very pulpit behind which you stood nearly fifty years ago. I also have the benefit of being held accountable by great men in our leadership who experienced some of the struggles of your time. They remember and remind me of the great sacrifices made by you and ultimately, by Christ. They remind me of the privilege and the responsibility I have to step up and be more courageous than cautious in the work of the kingdom. These men encourage me to move forward calling our Christian brothers and sisters out of waiting and away from being a "weak, ineffectual voice with an uncertain sound" toward an extreme idea . . . Christ-exalting diversity.

Thank you, Dr. King, for being a model and a mentor from afar and through the years.

I am grateful.

Pastor Charlie Dates

8

WHY WE CAN'T WAIT FOR CHRIST-EXALTING DIVERSITY

Charlie Dates

DR. KING WAS RIGHT. The struggle for racial equality and societal diversity is a church problem. He articulated that the problem was not with the extremist groups of Klansmen and citizens' councils but with the white Christian moderate. Albeit not the first to reach this conclusion, King detected a strange dichotomy between the message of Jesus Christ and the practice of His church in the American South.

It was white pastors who, while preaching the gospel, denied its power to the disinherited. It was predominantly the white Southern church pastors who further marginalized the disenfranchised by leveraging their collective rebellion against the ethics of the gospel in the cities where they preached. It was popular Christian practice to bar blacks from main floor seating in mainline churches in the South. It's ironic that "Bull" Conner, Birmingham's leading racist, its antagonist to freedom, and the commissioner for public safety had a striking biblical first name: Theophilus.[1]

To be sure today's American evangelicalism [Christianity] is yet unrepentant of its sin of segregation. There are, of course, notable exceptions. But some fifty years later, the sting of its sin is still felt in the curriculums of its affluent theological seminaries, it reverberates over the airwaves of its radio stations, and it resounds in the unchecked biases of its political commitments.

Dr. King's argument was not with the city of Birmingham but with the clergy in that city. His conflict was with those who knew the Scriptures. He fundamentally believed that the church had a moral obligation to undergird this movement. It was King's conviction that the movement needed those outside the black community to aid its cause, and that the only successful appeal for justice had to come on the basis of the Scripture. But instead of working together, according to Dr. King, the white Christian moderate was the greatest impediment to the movement.

Somewhat different than Dr. King's milieu, the problem today is not the white moderate as much as it is the Christian moderate of any race or stripe. The church seems to be a place where there is no room for what I call "missional moderation." By missional moderation I mean the institutional willingness to commit to the unfavorable, unwanted aspects of its mission. Fifty years later the American church is still slow to commit herself to the hard work of racial harmony. Five decades after this prison epistle, the faculties at our evangelical seminaries are still predominantly white men. I propose that our ecclesiastical hope for unity is still in jail.

Our challenge today remains an issue of Christian leadership. We suffer from leadership that regards particular biblical imperatives as options. To these leaders the imperatives for unity, harmony, and diversity seem better suited for the socially conscious than their own ecclesiological fellowships. To them it appears that part of the gospel is optional.

I'm arguing for the urgency and potency of Christ-exalting diversity. This essay's tenets rest upon theological and historical evidences to make its case. In this way, I want to intentionally detour from the trendy, often empty exploits of cultural diversity sought after in our schools, churches, boardrooms, and government today. I want to put forth a clarion call for biblical exposition on race and the gospel, the involvement of the marginalized in our Christian institutions, and a bolder, more aggressive attack on the lethargic pace at which the church is moving toward ethnic diversity.

Before building the case for the now-ness of Christ-exalting diversity, I want to remind you of a few things. Although not a Christian movement per se, the American civil rights movement of the 1930–70s was born out of the African American church.[2] More specifically, Dr. King was invited to Birmingham by Pastor Fred L. Shuttlesworth and the Alabama Christian Movement for Human Rights.[3] The movement was led primarily by black Baptist preachers. Its major anthropological (civil rights) claim was a more basic theological truth: all people, by virtue of being made in the image of God, are created equal. Diversity, therefore, is but an expression of the triune God.

We must recognize this at the outset because today's wider American movement for diversity is all but Christ-exalting. It is cotton candy diversity; puffed up, sweet air. It is the outworking of what the Irish playwright George Bernard Shaw once quipped, "God made us in His image and we returned the favor." The drive for diversity in America today exalts lifestyles that are incongruent with the *imago Dei*. I guess it is easy for those who do not yet know the liberating power of Jesus Christ to restrict the conversation of diversity to the exaltation of human depravity. Only Christ-exalting diversity respects and reclaims the image of God in mankind. It affirms every race and ethnicity, every woman and man regardless of social location.

We cannot wait for Christ-exalting diversity for four reasons. First—and perhaps most importantly—Christ-exalting diversity is God's idea. Secondly, Christ-exalting diversity is fundamental to the church's primary mission. Thirdly, Christ-exalting diversity most clearly illustrates and demonstrates the gospel of Jesus Christ. This kind of diversity is the boldest proclamation of the person and work of Jesus Christ available to the church in America today. And finally, Christ-exalting diversity is not trendy. It is prophetic.

CHRIST-EXALTING DIVERSITY IS GOD'S IDEA

We should not wait to bring about Christ-exalting diversity because the idea is thoroughly biblical. Dr. King considered his highest purpose to be a preacher of the gospel of Jesus Christ.[4] The underpinnings of both the civil rights movement and his letter from Birmingham were biblical ideas. In his Birmingham jail letter, Dr. King likens his response to help in Birmingham to Paul's vision to go help the Macedonians in Acts 16:9. He presents his case for civil disobedience by illustrating the refusal of Shadrach, Meshach, and Abednego to obey the laws of Nebuchadnezzer. When defending the appropriateness of their actions, King refers to Jesus' unique God-consciousness. Quoting Paul at 1 Corinthians 13, King describes his standing in the middle of two opposing Negro community forces, as the more excellent way of love. Finally, he contends that the prophets and even our Lord Jesus Christ were extremists.

The letter is laced with contextual use of Scripture. It was King who highlighted before an international audience the relationship between the yearning for freedom and the will of God for humankind. To him, if the mission for ethnic diversity is wrong, then God Almighty is wrong. From what biblical soil could he extract such an extreme idea? King developed his ideas from the Gospels, Paul, and the prophets. The Pauline epistles to the Ephesians and Corinthians grant to us the most persuasive case for the eradication of enmity between God and humankind, men and men, and the hope for reconciliation for humanity in Christ Jesus.

Paul's short epistle to the very literate and cosmopolitan city of Ephesus is perhaps the most compelling and convincing biblical case for Christ-exalting diversity. It is the story of the gospel in miniature. There is debate among scholars as to the primary purpose of Paul's letter to the Ephesians. Nonetheless, there is wide agreement that the dominant theme of the letter is the unity of the church.[5] Paul's argument is this: God's redemptive work in humankind was never to be limited to the small, provincial confines of one ethnicity. In fact, the expression of His love for all mankind was the ground from which the Gentile mission flowered. In one swift statement, Paul declares that Christ Himself is our peace.[6] Christ's death destroyed the hostility between humankind and created one new person by reconciling the Jew and Gentile factions.[7] Now fallen and extinct are the barriers that divided the Jewish community from the Gentiles. The church is, therefore, comprised of people from various ethnic backgrounds. Because of Christ's reconciling death, the temple no longer needed a wall to separate Jews from Gentiles. Christ's efficacious work on the cross made possible a new kind of church, the genuine fellowship between opposing ethnicities.

A basic misunderstanding of the gospel contributes to the unnecessary divisions among ethnic groups. In Ephesus Jewish and Gentile believers had to be told of their equality, their oneness in Christ, and of their unique singular mission. This oneness is established in the grace of God's reconciliation with fallen humanity. Whereas the Law of Moses excluded the Gentiles, now Christ's work fulfilled the Law and instituted a new body of believers that included both Jew and Gentile. Most striking about the Ephesians epistle is that the initiative for breaking down the barrier of the dividing wall is found solely in the person and work of Jesus Christ (Ephesians 2:11–16). Reconciliation was God's idea. The primary mission and message of Jesus Christ is one of reconciliation. He destroys the barriers that prohibit fellowship between humankind and God.

Paul's argument through his letters is consistent. His second letter to the church at Corinth adds a dimension to our understanding of reconciliation. Not only is God the initiator of reconciliation; He is the agent through which the reconciliation came. Paul tells us that it was God through Christ who reconciled the world to Himself. Simply put, God is the supply of His own demand. He himself has provided the means by which the very oneness that he desires for His church can be accomplished. It took God to reconcile God and mankind. And it takes God to reconcile men with men. But it gets better. God is not only the initiator and agent of reconciliation; He is also the goal of reconciliation (2 Corinthians 5:19). It is "to Himself" that the world is being reconciled. We can safely say that genuine reconciliation is all about God. It is a thoroughly biblical and theological concept.

On one hand Paul describes what the church is. On the other he describes the church's role in redemptive history. The church has the responsibility of both being and doing. We have been given the ministry of reconciliation, and are to simultaneously proclaim and demonstrate the reconciliatory accomplishment of God. Since God achieved reconciliation with man, so too the church is to participate in the mission of reconciliation to the world.

ANY DEFINITION of diversity that exchanges the exaltation of Christ for the exaltation of human depravity is insufficient.

We need look no further for an impetus to diversify our churches, schools, and boardrooms than the gospel itself. This is why genuine diversity must be Christ-exalting. Only in Christ do we have any hope for oneness. Only the miracle of the incarnation guarantees success in our approach toward one another across ethnic bounds. Only Christ makes us one body. Christ is the one hope of our calling. Christ is the one Lord. Could it be that this kind of harmony was on the mind of God the Father in the mission of Christ the Son? I think so. God always intended for His church to be made up of people of every kind of ethnic origin.

I am not saying that each homogenous church transgresses the boundaries of God's will. But I am strongly suggesting that every Christian entity ought to strive to be diverse in view of the person and work of Jesus Christ. Our being should determine our doing. Since the church universal is comprised of every nation, tongue, and tribe, the local fellowship of believers must give itself to the representation of that diversity.

To say that Christ-exalting diversity is God's idea is to say at the same time that there are other kinds of diversity that are not God's idea. As media coverage of the fiftieth anniversary of the March on Washington hit the airwaves, an unmistakable message circulated through America. The campaign for ethnic equality had been hijacked by the same-sex agenda. The struggle for civil rights in America is no longer an idea that exalts Christ because it longs to make righteous what God declares sinful. Any definition of diversity that exchanges the exaltation of Christ for the exaltation of human depravity is insufficient.

CHRIST-EXALTING DIVERSITY IS FUNDAMENTAL TO THE CHURCH'S PRIMARY MISSION

We cannot wait for Christ-exalting diversity because it is fundamental to our mission. The primary mission and message of Jesus Christ is the primary mission and message of His church. From my perch, it seems that my generation's struggle with the church is its attachment to abstract doctrine without a commitment to concrete action. There is a movement afoot within the American church that looks good but may prove dangerous later. A group of neoreformed diehards proclaim the central doctrines of the church unaccompanied by activity that demonstrates those doctrines. The church cannot afford to simply articulate doctrine. By its very nature she must display what she declares.

Hindrances to the successful completion of our mission abound. What has prompted failure in preceding generations is our unwillingness to apply the prerequisites of Christ-exalting diversity. Paul writes in 2 Corinthians 5:16 that we are to no longer recognize anyone according to the flesh. In the context of defining the ministry of reconciliation, Paul begins with a more basic instruction. We can no longer evaluate one another with the eyes of culture, prejudice, and the flesh. We now are to know no man after such criteria. Perhaps your experience is like mine. You have heard racial stereotypes from the most unlikely sources. Blacks do not trust whites. Whites think of blacks as impediments to their own progress. Other ethnic minorities are suspicious of one another. Whatever the misconceived idea of a racial group may be, it is forbidden as a lens through which we evaluate one another. As long as whites view black people as inferior, and black people harbor reasons for mistrust against whites, then we are "knowing" one another according to the flesh.

One way we can move forward in fulfilling the mission of a unified, diverse church that exalts the name of her Savior will require particular steps that display the efficacy of our doctrine. According to 2 Corinthians 5 we humans are obliged to respond to the offer of reconciliation. This is why the ambassador of verse 20 begs for action. Reconciliation is an offer with an offer. To be completely enacted, a response from the recipient is necessary. Here I attempt to chart a way forward. There must first be an admission of culpability for the racial division that now exists. And this admission must be both corporate and personal. Particular ethnic groups in America are the beneficiaries of racial segregation, societal prejudice, and historic injustices. Other ethnic groups in America are the payers for such privilege. The church in America needs to speak to these realities.

Second, the church must cease to pretend that the world's lack of diversity is a social problem separate from the sacred. Far too often the shared sentiment of biblical conservatives is what King called "a strange distinction between bodies and souls, the sacred and the secular." Our

WE SO DESPERATELY need Christian leaders who will no longer approve of the brokenness of culture being hidden away in the file of Christian indifference and irrelevance.

lack of Christ-exalting diversity is not first a social problem. It is a spiritual problem prompted by sin. Situated in his historical context, Dr. King said it best,

> I have heard numerous religious leaders of the South call upon their worshipers to comply with a desegregation decision because it is the law, but I have longed to hear white ministers say, follow this decree because integration is morally right and the Negro is your brother. In the midst of blatant injustices inflicted upon the Negro, I have watched white churches stand on the sidelines and merely mouth pious irrelevancies and sanctimonious trivialities. In the midst of a mighty struggle to rid our nation of racial and economic injustice, I have heard so many ministers say, "Those are social issues which the gospel has nothing to do with," and I have watched so many churches commit themselves to a completely otherworldly religion which made a strange distinction between bodies and souls, the sacred and the secular.[8]

The gospel has something to do with every facet of society, culture, and life. To proclaim otherwise is to preach an insufficient and erroneous gospel. We so desperately need Christian leaders who will no longer approve of the brokenness of culture being hidden away in the file of Christian indifference and irrelevance. Now is the time for a more "courageous than cautious" Christian leadership in America.

Now is the time for a group of Christian leaders who see the plight of society uniquely connected to the spiritual needs of humanity. History is the single greatest witness that the unbiblical distinction between the "social" and the ethics of the gospel is an excuse not to confront our own partnership with society's great racial evil. The church has participated in American racism. It continues to leave its assumptions of race unchecked and the effects of segregation unquestioned. It is slow to challenge the old, antiquated, soft-minded distinctions of what is social and what is spiritual.

Dr. King was right to call for a more tough-minded and tender-hearted church. This is the kind of church that possesses the mental fortitude to critically question its relationship with the world around it, and yet possesses the tenderness to care enough to act. In the first chapter of his book *Strength to Love*, King demonstrates the remarkable capacity to exegete big ideas in the Gospels. Expounding upon Jesus' commission to the Twelve, he hears a call for serpentlike wisdom and dovelike tenderness:

> Jesus recognized the need for blending opposites. He knew that his disciples would face a difficult and hostile world, where they would confront the recalcitrance of political officials and the intransigence of the protectors of the old order. He knew that they would meet cold and arrogant men whose hearts had been hardened by the long winter of traditionalism. So he said to them, "Behold, I send you forth as sheep in the midst of wolves," and he gave them a formula for action: "Be ye therefore wise as serpents, and harmless as doves."[9]

Building on the case for tough-mindedness, King identifies the dangers of soft-mindedness. He writes that the soft-minded are prone to embrace all kinds of superstitions. They always fear change, and quench the quest for truth. In the journey for freedom the church, he believed, needed more tough-minded people. "Jesus reminds us that the good life combines the toughness of the serpent and the tenderness of the dove. We as Negroes must bring together tough-mindedness and tenderheartedness, if we are to move creatively toward the goal of freedom and justice. Soft-minded individuals among us feel that the only way to deal with oppression is by adjusting to it. They acquiesce and resign themselves to segregation. They prefer to remain oppressed."[10]

In addition to the accommodation attitude of African Americans, King directed his criticism to the white Christian community that protected segregation by their soft-minded refusal to fight for justice because of their hard-heartedness. That problem yet exists today. We should call the lack of diversity in our Christian culture by its name: sin. Our sin is our insistence to enjoy the comforts of the status quo at the expense of a relevant testimony for Jesus Christ. Too often, the comfort of societal sin has contributed to the growth and success of segments of the church. Large, affluent, homogenous Christian organizations must wrestle with how the fallenness of America's race-based culture has contributed to their prosperity. Then we must have the tenderheartedness to do something with the conclusions of our wrestling.

Third, when the church sees the unique relationship between the social problems and spiritual solutions, it must move toward Christ-exalting diversity *now*. Time can give the allusion that more of it is available than actually exists. It can make us believe that within its banks is the currency for our solutions. This is what King meant when he spoke of his hopes that the white moderate would reject the myth of time.

It is the strangely irrational notion that there is something in the very flow of time that will inevitably cure all ills. Actually, time is neutral. It can be used either destructively or constructively. I am coming to feel that the people of ill will have used time much more effectively than the people of good will. We will have to repent in this generation not merely for the vitriolic words and actions of the bad people but for the appalling silence of the good people. We must come to see that human progress never rolls in on wheels of inevitability. It comes through the tireless efforts and persistent work of men willing to be coworkers with God; and without this hard work time itself becomes an ally of the forces of social stagnation."[11]

King's generation is not the only one that will need to repent for its poor stewardship of the moment. Ours may have to do the same. The failures of previous generations to bring about diversity that exalts Christ heightens the urgency for our contemporary culture.

CHRIST-EXALTING DIVERSITY MOST CLEARLY ILLUSTRATES THE GOSPEL OF JESUS CHRIST

I firmly believe that our Christian witness is at stake. When governments and universities that don't bear the name of Jesus Christ are the most active pursuers of diversity, the church loses a measure of relevance in the life of the broader culture. That irrelevance is compounded when from one generation to the next the sloth of pursuit thickens. Dr. King noticed the hazardous, dangerous path of irrelevance upon which his generation of the church trod. "The contemporary church," he wrote,

> is so often a weak, ineffectual voice with an uncertain sound. It is so often the arch supporter of the status quo. Far from being disturbed by the presence of the church, the power structure of the average community is consoled by the church's often vocal sanction of things as they are. But the judgment of God is upon the church as never before. If the church of today does not recapture the sacrificial spirit of the early church, it will

lose its authentic ring, forfeit the loyalty of millions, and be dismissed as an irrelevant social club with no meaning for the twentieth century. I meet young people every day whose disappointment with the church has risen to outright disgust.[12]

I know a little something about an irrelevant church. In my city, more and more churches are reaching the hundred-year mark with several of their parishioners not far from that year themselves. More and more young people are abandoning the church of their fathers for no other sacred alternative. In the neighborhood where I serve, churches are growing older, slower, and more unattractive. It is not because the timeless story of the gospel is unattractive or unappealing but because many of the neighborhood churches have lost their incarnational vernacular. It is as though we have forgotten that the incarnation itself is not only a miracle but also a method of communication. Young people are hungry for a church that speaks prophetically to culture.

My college pastor used to say that the church at its birth was the church at its best. I wanted so desperately to prove him wrong. The "Letter from a Birmingham Jail" echoes similar sentiments. Dr. King saw in the early church a certain riskiness and boldness. Of those days, he said the church was not simply a thermometer that registered popular opinion but a thermostat that transformed society. How else can you describe the church in Acts 13? Here is one church in one city, Antioch, comprised of leaders of multiple ethnicities. What must it have been like to be part of a church whose prophets and teachers were Barnabas, Simeon who was called Niger, and Lucius of Cyrene? The church at its birth demonstrated the power of the gospel to bridge racial, cultural chasms.

What clearer illustration of the gospel of Jesus Christ is available to young Americans today than that of a Christ-exalting diverse church? The young professionals at our church work with whites, Asians, Latinos, and African Americans. They shop at stores with them. They attend conferences with them. They visit hospitals with them, but do not go to church with them. It is seemingly the one significant area of ecclesiastical lag. Our coming together, despite our ethnic differences, preaches a sermon by itself. Our doing life together demonstrates that Jesus Christ is the only person who can make brothers of enemies. Our coming together says that there is something universal about Christian brotherhood without regard to ethnicity. It preaches the power of Jesus.

CHRIST-EXALTING DIVERSITY
IS PROPHETIC, NOT TRENDY

A resurgence of conversation regarding prophetic preaching is growing in a few African American homiletical circles. They are exploring questions like, What is prophetic preaching? What does it mean to preach prophetically? How can the church preach truth to power? It is a noble and fascinating discussion. I guess the success of these conversations will depend on what is meant by prophecy. All preaching should be prophetic in the forth-telling of truth if not in the foretelling of truth.

What has become a trend is supposed to be the mainstay of the church. Our message is still prophetic. Dr. King regularly quoted the Old Testament Minor Prophets. In his letter from Birmingham, King quickly referenced Amos and situated him in the category of extremity. We have to admit that the prophetic message is not only one of urgency but also one of extremity. None of the Old Testament prophets was welcomed as a hometown hero. Jeremiah walked around in shameful rags. Elijah lived under the constant threat of death with a hit out on his life issued by the king's wife. Hosea had a public relationship with a less-than-faithful wife. Nahum was anything but comfort to Nineveh. Each of their lives were burdened with a sense of urgency and extremity. Their messages, though unpopular, were direct from the throne room of heaven. They testify to us that God's activity in the world is packaged in urgency and extremity.

Christ-exalting diversity is an extreme idea. Like the prophetic message, it will not always be embraced with enthusiasm. Very often, it will be abandoned for an easier agenda. Whether or not the church intentionally moves toward this diversity may be the telling sign for the future of the church in America. If we read this book and cast the idea aside, we spell failure for future generations. But if we trust God enough to take the risk of reconciliation, we empower future generations to go further than we've dreamed.

I conclude with this story. The twelve-year-old boy stood in front of eight hundred congregants, poised to deliver his lines. His assignment was to recite extensive portions of Dr. King's "Letter from a Birmingham Jail." The elementary school principal of that south side Christian academy would not let the eighth graders graduate without first committing to memory large swaths of King's writings. Over and again he had said those lines, swallowed those ideas before his home audience of mother and brothers until that moment came. As the little boy stepped to the microphone, the congregation grew still while his heart pounded the drum of palpable energy. That moment could not speak more of his future ministry. He opened his mouth to say, "For years now I have heard the word 'wait.' It rings in the ear of every Negro with a piercing familiarity. This 'wait' has almost always meant 'never.'"

Only God knew what the future held for that young boy. It is now twenty-nine years later and he serves as the senior pastor of Chicago's historic Progressive Baptist Church. He is privileged to preach from the very pulpit behind which King stood in Chicago nearly fifty years ago. Every now and then a few of our deacons remind me of visions they've seen of this historically black congregation growing into a vibrant multiracial fellowship of believers. They encourage me to move forward. I stand in front of that congregation and do as I encourage you. I call our church out of waiting toward an extreme idea: Christ-exalting diversity.

Dear Dr. King,

I was in my early twenties when I first read the letter you wrote while in jail in Birmingham. At that time my heart had already been marked by your passion and vision for diversity. I'd already been stirred to pursue a lifelong journey in the participation of "the dream" you spoke about and to spend my days, my life, and the influence God had given me, to see that dream come true.

When I read your letter I wept, my resolve growing stronger as I came to the end. Whatever God had for me in the future, I would learn from those of different ethnicities and have as many deep and diverse friendships as possible, while guarding against the ignorance birthed in homogeny.

As a white man born to white parents, living under the privilege of the dominant culture, staying this path hasn't been easy. Whenever I have hit bumps in the road as the pastor of a large church, I find myself drawn back to your passion, vision, and sacrifice for the cause of multiethnic harmony and the type of diversity that brings glory to God and sanctifies men.

Diversity that is not simply an assembly of multiraced but assimilated peoples can only be done through God's grace and the power of the Holy Spirit. This is what my heart is hungry for.

I am grateful for the course you charted, in your service to Christ. I am praying the Spirit of God would guide our steps today as we seek to better display His love for all men. And I seek to continue learning from my brothers of other ethnicities.

For your passion and vision for diversity and humility, thank you, Dr. King.

> Faithfully devoted to Christ in the journey.
> Your brother,
> **Pastor Matt Chandler**

9

THE TIME IS NOW FOR MULTIETHNIC CHURCHES AND MOVEMENTS

Matt Chandler

". . . SUCH AN ATTITUDE stems from a tragic misconception of time, from the strangely irrational notion that there is something in the very flow of time that will inevitably cure all ills. Actually, time itself is neutral; it can be used either destructively or constructively."[1]

We've been waiting hundreds of years for the Western church to become more diverse and mirror our brother and sisters in the first century, where the Christian church stood out as a beacon of beautiful bright light illuminating the distinct value and worth of every human being created in the image of God. The hope that the next generation will usher in the gathering of people from different cultures, socioeconomic stations, and colors under one roof to worship has been just that: a hope for the future, consistently punted down the field of history.

But we can no longer push diversity on the next generation, asking our children to be obedient in an area we are not. We can no longer wait for our churches to magically become more ethnically diverse and continue to punt this issue down the field of history. The world is ripe to see and marvel at the gospel's power to break down walls of hostility and heal historic mistrust, misunderstanding, and anger. In the growing heat of marginalization, let us be refined from the many to the one. We need men and women of courage to lead us into humility and help navigate us through the difficulties of this pursuit. It will not be quick or easy; but it is necessary. This pursuit will require vision that isn't built upon shortsighted white guilt or paternalistic rescue. It will need to be much more than blacks, whites, Latinos, Asians, and Indians being in the same room together. It must be the new community of faith that God has designed His people to walk in.

To be clear, diversity is not on par with the gospel. Many good-hearted brothers and sisters have elevated this issue to the level of gospel, and I find that tragic. To make these two issues the same issue is an error that will ensure that our hope for multiethnic congregations will fail. Diversity is an implication and hope fueled by the gospel, but it is not the good news. Yet, while the gospel and diversity are not equal ideas, diversity is nevertheless an issue that we are weak in and need to grow in—an issue that requires much time, energy, and prayer.

The community I grew up in was not predominantly Anglo. In fact, looking through my yearbook, it would be hard for anyone to explain the dominant race. It was right before my senior year of high school that Jesus saved me through the ministry of a church that sat directly across the street from my high school's football stadium. On Friday nights, our diverse community of white-collar managers and blue-collar workers and Asians, Anglos, African Americans, Hispanics, and Indians would use the church's parking lot for overflow. The parking lot and that stadium on Friday nights looked completely different than that same parking lot and the church on Sunday mornings. On Sunday mornings, that parking lot—like the worship center and Sunday school rooms—was filled with only Anglos. The church wasn't "Anglo only," and none of the members considered themselves racists. They had friends and neighbors of different ethnicities; but for whatever reason, every Sunday our community that shared in education, sports, neighborhoods, and other community celebrations chose to worship the same God in segregated silos.

What I am describing probably doesn't shock anyone. This is normative for evangelicals. Because I was blessed to not grow up in a homogenized community, I didn't even recognize the oddity of segregated Sunday mornings. However, most of us don't recognize the homogeny we are walking in because every area of our lives, neighborhoods, and schools is predominately one color and one culture. When this takes place, the way we see the world becomes dangerously narrow and puts us at odds with God's redemptive design for all peoples. For all of the church's current weaknesses, homogenization proves most visible, affects us most negatively, and shapes so many of our other weaknesses that it screams to be addressed in our day.

So where do we start to address this issue? How do we stop pushing it to the next generation of believers? How do we humbly and courageously pursue diversity in our churches? I think a good start is seeing the issue through the lenses of theology, philosophy, and practice. For the purpose of this chapter, I want to look especially at a theology of diversity because *theology* is the foundation of the house, and the foundation must obviously come first. Without a strong foundation, the whole house becomes weak and at risk of collapsing. It doesn't matter what the house may look like if the foundation is shaky. Whether the house is custom-built or one of four choices in a cookie-cutter neighborhood, the foundation is still crucial, and its importance cannot be overstated. More specifically, the foundation must be the timeless and true Word of God. In the Scriptures, we clearly discover the glorious gospel, the great metanarrative, the grand story of redemption.[2]

THEOLOGY

The hope for an ethnically diverse church comes in the power of the gospel, but the root of diversity exists in the triune nature of God. The doctrine of the Trinity is that God is one being who exists eternally in three persons: Father, Son, and Holy Spirit. When describing the inner workings of the Trinity, the early church fathers used the term *perichoresis*, an ancient Greek word capturing the ideas of relational perimeters (peri-"around" + *chorein*- "to contain") and movement (*peri*-"around" + *khoreuo*-"dance"). The persons of the Trinity interpenetrate while remaining distinct and self-contained. "The Father . . . Son . . . and Holy Spirit glorify each other . . . At the center of the universe, self giving love is the dynamic currency of the Trinitarian life of God. The persons within God exalt, commune with, and defer to one another. . . . When early Greek Christians spoke of perichoreis in God they meant that each divine person harbors the other at the center of his being. In constant movement of overture and acceptance each person envelopes and encircles the others."[3] This means that the Godhead is in perfect, beautiful community. God is in His essence relational.

> **WHEN WE ARE transfixed on similarities, we make others a mirror of ourselves. Other people are simply a part of our own worlds, objects of our own experiences.**

The Godhead is diverse. The Father, Son, and Holy Spirit relate to each other personally. The Father regards Himself as "I," while He regards the Son and Holy Spirit as "You." Likewise, the Son regards Himself as "I," but the Father and Holy Spirit as "You."[4] They are distinct, diverse persons, yet one God. At creation God says: *Let us make man in our image, after our likeness* and then again *it is not good that the man should be alone.* We see here that God created man in His image to be in relationship because God is in His essence relational. The relationship God builds for Adam is completely distinct from Adam, revealing what we know to be true. All relationships are diverse. Human beings, by virtue of their humanity, are diverse, and it is in the sharing of lives that people are most human.

THE FALL

Before sin fractures the cosmos, the picture of diverse human relationship is one of being different yet "naked and unashamed." A harmony in differences evaporated in the fall. When sin entered the picture, the harmony became replaced by self-seeking, self-worshiping sinfulness. Now that sin rules the lives of men and women, we naturally seek similarities in human relationships instead of differences. As a basis for interaction, we seek to find common ground. On the surface, it seems appropriate or, in the least, efficient to do so. Self-interested individuals meet more goals when faced with less opposition. When sinful self-interested individuals assemble, Babel-like towers to heaven are only the "beginning of what they can do." Many, eager to make a name for themselves, use their fellow man, considering them objects— a collective means to an individual end. Because this self-centeredness is outside God's creative design, He, in every moment, reveals diversity to confuse the progress and to crumble monuments to self. Other persons provide an opportunity to experience unselfish ambitions and fullness of life. Differences are a gift woven into the fabric of creation designed to free individuals from their inward captivity.

Relationships fail, typically, not because of a lack of appreciating similarities but a disregard for important, God-given differences. People are diverse in every way, and that diversity enriches relationships, humbles hearts, and lines us up with God's creative design. When we are transfixed on similarities, we make others a mirror of ourselves. Other people are simply a part of our own worlds, objects of our own experiences. It is when a person is encountered as a subject—a real person—that differences become obvious and ultimately a blessing.[5] What can save us then from our desire of self-seeking and self-worshiping into the freedom that God has for us?

THE GOSPEL: THE POWER FOR DIVERSITY

There is a consistent rhythm throughout the Scriptures that God's plan is to form a people of every tribe, tongue, and nation on earth. Revelation 7 gets the most mention, but it simply paints a picture of the culmination of God's redemptive work in history. We see the first promise to accomplish the picture of Revelation 7 in Genesis 12:3 when God tells Abram that "all the families of the earth shall be blessed." We see it in Exodus 9:16 when God says, "I have raised you up for this very purpose . . . that my name might be proclaimed in all the earth" (NIV). Numbers 14:21 says, *the glory of God fills the whole earth*, while Deuteronomy 28:10 (NASB) says, *all the peoples of the earth will see that you are called by the name of the Lord*. From Joshua to Malachi, there are dozens and dozens of verses used to discuss global missions. God's plan isn't just to redeem and save from among all tribes, tongues, and nations, but his plan is to make a people out of them.

The coming of Jesus Christ sealed the fate of homogeny once and for all. We find pointed and powerful words in Paul's epistle to the church at Ephesus that help us see how the gospel creates a new people out of individuals from all peoples, socioeconomic places, and cultural nuance. Ephesians 2:11–20 says:

> Therefore remember that at one time you Gentiles in the flesh, called "the uncircumcision" by what is called the circumcision, which is made in the flesh by hands—remember that you were at that time separated from Christ, alienated from the commonwealth of Israel and strangers to the covenants of promise, having no hope and without God in the world. But now in Christ Jesus you who once were far off have been brought near by the blood of Christ. For he himself is our peace, who has made us both one and has broken down in his flesh the dividing wall of hostility by abolishing the law

of commandments expressed in ordinances, that he might create in himself one new man in place of the two, so making peace, and might reconcile us both to God in one body through the cross, thereby killing the hostility. And he came and preached peace to you who were far off and peace to those who were near. For through him we both have access in one Spirit to the Father. So then you are no longer strangers and aliens, but you are fellow citizens with the saints and members of the household of God, built on the foundation of the apostles and prophets, Christ Jesus himself being the cornerstone.

The life, death, and resurrection of Jesus Christ have accomplished something spectacular for those considered aliens and strangers to the ethnic Jews of the first century. Peter states in Acts 10:28 that it was *unlawful for a Jew to associate with or visit anyone of another nation.* That's hostility. It sounds like some of the Jim Crow laws that existed in the Southern states only a few decades ago. This hostility views one culture and people group as superior and of greater value than another group. It dehumanizes and marginalizes a whole people group. Almost all segregation, oppression, genocide, and ethnic cleansing stems from the hostility that Paul addresses here. The imagery of "walls" is piercing and focused.

In the Herodian temple of the first century, there were multiple courts before one arrived in the inner court, which was only accessible to Jewish men in right standing according to the laws and customs of that day. Gentiles were allowed to go no farther that the outermost court. After that court, there was a court for Jewish women and then finally the inner court. Archaeologists found an inscription on the outer court wall that was put up as a warning to the Gentiles. The inscription read, "Whoever is captured will have himself to blame for his subsequent death." This isn't happening in some backwoods country town;

this is in the Herodian temple in the heart of Jerusalem. The Scriptures teach us that the person and work of Jesus Christ have torn down these walls. They should no longer exist.

Paul goes on to describe how thoroughly God demolished this nonsense, and the way He tears down the walls by His blood should cause a holy hush to fall on all of us. The apostle writes that Jesus created *in himself one new man in place of the two, so making peace, and might reconcile us both to God in one body through the cross, thereby killing the hostility*. God has taken the Jews (with their covenant promises, ordinances, and the law) and the Gentiles (who represented every other color, culture, and class and were alienated and considered second-class citizens, unworthy to be in close proximity to the holiness of God) and makes them together a new people. Those who were viewed as clean were made one with those viewed as unclean. They were formed into something together that the Bible calls "new."

The word "new" here is the Greek word *Kainos*. It is one of two Greek words for new, and it means "of a new kind, unprecedented, novel, uncommon, unheard of." To quote a friend of mine, "this isn't the new 2013 Ford Explorer; this is the Model T." The church at Ephesus is getting a lesson in diversity. God builds on the foundation of the apostles and prophets a new people made up of every tribe, tongue, nationality, color, culture, and class imaginable with Jesus as the cornerstone to hold it all together.

We see this diversity as the norm of New Testament church planting and community. The Spirit planted and built multiethnic churches that stood out and against the prevailing thoughts of the day. This "newness" was both difficult and beautiful, as we see the conversion of Cornelius: *While Peter was still saying these things, the Holy Spirit fell on all who heard the word. And the believers from among the circumcised who had come with Peter were amazed, because the gift of the Holy Spirit was poured out even on the Gentiles. For they were hearing them speaking in tongues and extolling God. Then Peter declared, "Can anyone withhold water for baptizing these people, who have received the Holy Spirit just as we have?" And he commanded them to be baptized in the name of Jesus Christ. Then they asked him to remain for some days* (Acts 10:44–48).

How amazing is this? God's plan for creating a "new" people is starting; but it's not without its critics. Two verses later (11:2–3), we read: *So when Peter went up to Jerusalem, the circumcision party criticized him, saying, "You went to uncircumcised men and ate with them."* God does the miraculous, and there are Christians frustrated that Peter went to a non-Jew's house and had the audacity to eat with them. The "new" that God was bringing in wasn't an easy transition to make for many who had grown up in a predominate culture believing they were superior.

After this account, the Christian Jews who were scattered by persecution were sharing the gospel, which is commendable but look at Acts 11:19–21: *Now those who were scattered because of the persecution that arose over Stephen traveled as far as Phoenicia and Cyprus and Antioch,* **speaking the word to no one except Jews.** *But there were some of them, men of Cyprus and Cyrene, who on coming to Antioch spoke to the Hellenists also, preaching the Lord Jesus. And the hand of the Lord was with them, and a great number who believed turned to the Lord.* This is exactly what we fight through today: we are drawn to sameness by our sinfulness and self-righteousness, yet God is calling us into differences for His glory and our good.

When the apostle Paul is called to church planting, God's plan for a multiethnic community of faith shifts into fifth gear. The Holy Spirit in Acts 13 calls Paul out of the church at Antioch, and even the room he is in at the time is a diverse one. We read in verse 1 that "Now there were in the church at Antioch prophets and teachers, Barnabas, Simeon who was called Niger, Lucius of Cyrene, Manaen a lifelong friend of Herod the tetrarch, and Saul." There are different colors, cultures, and stations represented in the room mentioned above, but all are praying and fasting—all are brothers in Christ. As Paul set out to fulfill his calling, we watch him operate in a specific way: When he comes to town, he starts at synagogues, teaching and reasoning with those who are of the same race and culture as himself, but he doesn't stop there. In Athens, he starts in the synagogue and ends up reasoning at Mars Hill, and the result is a church in Athens made up of both Jews and Gentiles. In Ephesus, Paul starts in the synagogue and ends up in the Hall of Tyrannus where he *reasoned for two years so that all the residents of Asia heard the word of the Lord, both Jews and Greeks.* If you think back over Ephesians 2:11–20, that church must have been struggling with the differences in ethnic preferences, mindsets, approaches to life, etc., because Paul reminds them that the hostility is over and they are now one. He tells them to show deference, be patient and gracious, realize that you are family and fight for peace.

Our motivation for diversity and multiethnic congregations and networks isn't based on a whim. We haven't pulled it from thin air. It matters to us because it matters to God. It's God's plan that He will accomplish, and He has invited us to participate in what He will most certainly do. Yet, it will take more than a correct theology of diversity to participate in God's design; it will require a philosophy and an understanding of how to practice that philosophy.

PHILOSOPHY

A church or network is healthy when there is congruence and consistency between what they say is important and what others know *really is* important to her. If a church declares that the gospel is the most important message the world has ever known and yet the gospel is not seen as the impetus and motivation for all the church offers, this disconnect proves indicative of an unhealthy church personality or culture. Likewise, a church with a theology of diversity but no philosophy or practice of diversity will never see the fruit of what they believe.

So what does a philosophy of diversity look like? If our doctrine says that all men and women are created in the image of God and that differences are good and will shape and mold us into the image of Christ, one key aspect of the philosophy is the intrinsic value of learning from those of different backgrounds and cultures. Thus, we should dive headfirst into seeking to understand our cultural and ethnic differences. Whether it is musical style, dress, language, or the way preaching is handled, we should seek to understand these differences. The key is looking into these differences with a desire to learn and grow from what we find and not from a posture of personal preference or a perceived position of superiority. There is no longer—for the believer—a "predominant culture." We must fight against this notion and work at discovering and practicing the "new man" culture that our heavenly Father purchased for us by the blood of His Son. We must seek out and learn from our brothers and sisters, regardless of background or ethnicity. The Anglo who likes a more "Anglo" style of worship will have to seek to understand the more celebratory worship of African Americans and Latinos and likewise. One way isn't better than the other; and we must always be willing to try and understand, seek clarity charitably, and defer often for the good of the community of faith and the glory of God. Regardless of where your ministry plays out with all its contextual nuances, this aspect will have to be a philosophy of your ministry. Seek understanding and shared learning.

In the desire to build a diverse ministry, another aspect of your philosophy must be the desire to war against old patterns of self-seeking and self-worshiping sinfulness. It is a rare thing for me in my context to come across someone who admits to being racist. The politically correct demands of the Dallas/Fort Worth metroplex push vocal racists to the margins. However, while the demands of political correctness

> **BY NEGLECTING the practice part of the equation, a church can have a great doctrinal statement in place and philosophical thinkers sitting around discussing intellectually how ministry should be performed without ever actually doing it.**

might change how we talk, they won't change our hearts. It's so easy to drift back into the safety and efficiency of homogeny, and we see this vibrantly in Galatians 2:11–14: *But when Cephas came to Antioch, I opposed him to his face, because he stood condemned. For before certain men came from James, he was eating with the Gentiles; but when they came he drew back and separated himself, fearing the circumcision party, and the rest of the Jews. . . . But when I saw that their conduct was not in step with the truth of the gospel, I said to Cephas before them all, "If you, though a Jew, live like a Gentile and not like a Jew, how can you force the Gentiles to live like Jews?"* Multiethnic ministry will require us to frequently fight against the pull back to what is "easier" and what lines up more with our personal preferences.

One last aspect of a philosophy of diversity that must be in place is the celebration of differences. The Bible teaches that difference is good. The Godhead is many but one. All human relationships are diverse, so we should celebrate diversity in a way that praises God for the good gift of differences.

PRACTICE

From philosophy comes practice, and this aspect is critical because it's what people in a church interact with on an ongoing basis. Many churches practice ministry haphazardly, revealing that competing ministry philosophies are embedded into different segments of the church. By neglecting the practice part of the equation, a church can have a great doctrinal statement in place and philosophical thinkers sitting around discussing intellectually how ministry should be performed without ever actually doing it.[6]

"We have sought out, empowered, and equipped different ethnicities at the highest levels of our organization." We agree with our brother John Piper that it is a good thing to consider race when hiring. To his critics he responded:

> To the degree that one of the aims of an organization is to experience and display racial diversity, to that degree the intentional consideration of race in hiring is warranted. If, for example, the sole aim of an organization is productive efficiency, it would be unwarranted for the hiring guidelines to contain racial preferences. Whether all the employees are Black or Asian or White or Latino or Native is irrelevant. All that matters is maximum efficiency. So you don't consider race in hiring. The only thing you consider is competencies that maximize efficiency.
>
> However, if a stated aim of an organization is to experience and display the beauty of ethnic harmony in diversity, it is reasonable and warranted to consider race as part of the qualifications in hiring. An obvious example would be hiring actors for a dramatic production that includes African American, Asian, Latino, and Anglo roles. The producer or director would consider race essential in the actors hired for each role. That individual would not say that competency in acting is the only thing that matters and then use makeup to create the impression of race. Hence, it is reasonable and warranted to take ethnicity into account when hiring actors."[7]

This practice is tied back to the philosophy of learning from and seeking understanding and input from those who are different.

At the Village Church and in the Acts 29 Network, we have developed the practice of getting feedback from different ethnic groups on everything from music, retreats, websites, and sermons. This practice has not always changed what we were pursuing, but many times it has. This goes back to our philosophy of learning from each other and showing deference to others.

At The Village, we have celebrated diversity with what we call "musical diversity month," where we change our style of worship from week to week and remind the people that God loves diversity and difference and we must be willing to lay aside personal preference and celebrate those differences. This practice is tied back to reminding our people that we have a tendency to drift back to homogeny and must fight against it.

There are many other practices that can be mixed into the life of your church, but let us passionately pursue consistency between what we believe the Bible teaches, the philosophy of applying that truth, and then the application or practice itself.

CONCLUSION

One of the great joys I've had as a pastor and leader is learning from other pastors and leaders. That learning has taken place in a multitude of ways. I've learned from men who differ from me in theology and practice, and I've learned from those who differ in philosophy and culture. The friends the Lord has graciously gifted to me over these past eleven years are staggering, and I'm grateful for each and every one of them. Nowhere have I learned more than when I am with men of a different ethnicity who share the same doctrinal understandings that I do. When I have had a meal or a cup of coffee with Eric Mason in Philadelphia, Doug Logan in Camden, Bryan Loritts in Memphis,

Bryan Carter in Dallas, Leonce Crump in Atlanta, or Lorenzo Elizondo in Oak Cliff, I find the Spirit of God churning my heart to see more of His glory in and through a bold ethnic harmony that reveals God's glory and the power of the gospel in a visual and captivating way.

One of my burning hopes for the Village Church and the Acts 29 Church Planting Network is that we might boldly and unapologetically become a radically diverse crowd in our day. I refuse to punt the fight for this to my children and the next generation of pastors without giving myself over to what the Lord has asked me to pursue. Diversity is core to being explicitly Christian. The Scriptures teach that there are two races, the race of the first Adam and the race of the second. It's only in Christ that we are able to find our core identity. Our different cultures carry history, traditions, and legacies, but the gospel transcends all that and makes us a new people, a family. We continue to value what is good and right in our cultures but submit gladly to the new family as adopted sons and coheirs of Christ.

The cross of Calvary isn't theoretical—it changes how we view ourselves and others. It alone can heal wounds and create brotherly affections and direction. It destroys the walls of hostility. Producing homogenous churches can be done with relative ease and a total lack of dependence on the Spirit. That's not what I'm hopeful for. Diversity that is not simply an assembly of multiraced but assimilated peoples can only be done through God's grace and the power of the Holy Spirit. This is what my heart is hungry for. I'm praying the Spirit of God would guide our steps as we seek to better display His love for all man. We can't wait any longer. The time is now!

Dear Dr. King,

As a child growing up in a Korean American church, I was blessed to encounter Christians from the majority culture, many of whom contributed to my spiritual formation. As a college and seminary student, and as a young church planter, I was blessed to be mentored by African American, Latino/a, and Native American Christians who spoke truth into my life.

Micah 4 raises the promise of a racially reconciled multiethnic community. As I reflect on your letter through the lens of Micah 4, I am reminded that, in Christ, I no longer have to live under an oppressive system of segregation separating me from my brothers and sisters. Instead, I have the privilege of engaging across the dividing walls of hostility and finding a spiritual vibrancy in a restored Christian community.

This vision of the unified church, promised in Micah 4 and birthed in Acts 2, will culminate in Revelation 7:9 (NIV) with "a great multitude that no one could count, from every nation, tribe, people, and language standing before the throne and before the Lamb." The challenge before our church today, as in your time, is how to fully live into the promise of Micah 4.

While we continue to experience the blessings and challenges of diversity in our nation, one significant characteristic stubbornly extends into our time: 11 a.m. Sunday morning remains the most segregated hour in the nation. As we consider building more multiethnic churches, the work of confronting racial injustices by pursuing racial reconciliation and biblical justice becomes all the more important.

It's a hard and sacrificial work as you well know. May the church seize this moment to respond to your challenge and fulfill the biblical call to a true multiethnic community of worship.

Your brother in the pursuit,

Soong-Chan Rah

10

A MORE BIBLICAL SUNDAY MORNING

Soong-Chan Rah

INTRODUCTION

WHEN DR. KING penned the "Letter from a Birmingham Jail," his world differed vastly from our current twenty-first-century context. Many things have changed for the better over the course of several decades, including legislation that affirms the dignity and rights of African Americans. Our nation continues to experience both the blessing and challenges of diversity. One salient characteristic among many others, however, stubbornly extends into our time: 11 a.m. Sunday morning remains the most segregated hour in the United States.

This ongoing segregation stands in stark contrast to the demographic realities of Christianity throughout the world and in the United States. By the close of the twentieth century, the majority of Christians in the world no longer resided on the continents of North America and Europe. The two continents that have dominated global Christianity for centuries were now fading in light of the spectacular growth of the church in Africa, Asia, and Latin America. One estimate asserts that by 2025 an overwhelming percentage (75 percent) of Christians in the world will reside outside of Europe and North America.[1] Philip Jenkins offers a colorful illustration by claiming that "soon, the phrase 'a White Christian' may sound like a curious oxymoron, as mildly surprising as 'a Swedish Buddhist.'"

The drastic change in the demographics of world Christianity is also evident in the demographics of American Christianity. Increasing diversity in the US church reflects the diversity of American society. Changing demographics in the United States have resulted in the proliferation of immigrant churches throughout the country. Driving through a Washington, DC, suburb, a careful observer will note that many older church buildings with a church sign in English out front, will have a sign in Korean directly underneath. A visit to any major city reveals a large number of Spanish-speaking storefront churches scattered throughout the city. The increase in the number of immigrant churches is expanding the type of churches in the United States. In light of these dramatic shifts, how has the church in the United States changed and what are the present and future challenges for the church in the United States?

This chapter examines the current social/historical context of American Christianity and addresses the challenges in fulfilling the vision of a multiethnic church in our current social and ecclesial reality. We will also examine the challenge of the biblical call and mandate to pursue multiethnic congregations. And finally, we will examine how Dr. King's words in his letter from the Birmingham jail challenge us to move toward the possibility of a biblical multiethnic community.

HOW THE WORLD, THE COUNTRY, AND THE CHURCH HAVE CHANGED

From the advent of the civil rights movement to our current twenty-first-century multiethnic context, the evangelical church remained largely disconnected from many of the racial issues that engulfed our culture. Historian Curtis Evans notes that white evangelical Protestants were among "King's fiercest critics." Evans notes that "evangelicals were opposed to the civil rights movement and did very little in practical terms to advance social justice for African Americans during the 1960s."[2] Evangelical churches have been conspicuously absent from the voices that called for racial justice, but at the same time, we have not been immune to the demographic and cultural changes that have occurred around us. Our society has adapted to these changes and the evangelical church has observed and even benefitted from these changes.

For example, changes in the laws that emerged out of the civil rights movement benefited the entirety of American society by introducing a more just and fair system in the United States. The civil rights movement, therefore, led to a more just society and in turn, benefited the church in the context of civic society. One of the key outcomes of the movement was the Immigration and Nationality Act of 1965, which rearranged the quota system that favored immigrants from Europe. The quota system limiting immigration remained, but the distribution within that quota system opened the door for the influx of immigrants from Asia, Latin America, and Africa.

The 1965 legislation led to dramatic changes in the demographics of US society. Since 1965, there has been a steady rise in the ethnic minority population in the United States. My family personally benefited from the changes in the immigration laws in 1965. In 1973, our Korean family immigrated to the United States and eventually became US citizens, embracing our identity as Korean Americans. Over the last several decades, many foreign born families have made the choice that our family made. The US Census projects that "the minority population is expected to increase to the point that they represent the numeric majority between 2040 and 2050."[3]

This demographic trend propels the church in the United States toward increased diversity. Initially, sociologists believed that the influx of non-European immigrants would lead to a decline of Christianity in the United States. Sociologist R. Stephen Warner notes that "we should recognize that the extent of the new religious and racial diversity in the United States is unprecedented but also not forget that most of the new immigrants are Christian."[4] Many of the immigrants are indeed bringing a deep faith to the shores of the United States but it happens to be a deep Christian faith. When our family arrived in the United States, we immediately became involved in a Korean immigrant church. We were surrounded by other immigrant families who supported our transition to life in a foreign land. The church provided social services and a spiritual community that helped us to maintain our Christian faith in the transitional journey from Korea to the United States.

Warner recognizes, therefore, that the "new immigrants represent not the de-Christianization of American society but the de-Europeanization of American Christianity."[5] This new form of American Christianity is exemplified by the increasing presence of Asian Americans in evangelical seminaries, increased church planting efforts in evangelical denominations by Latinos, the replacing of aging, white churches with immigrant churches, and increased participation in white churches by African Americans.[6]

Diversity in the makeup of American Christianity, however, has not necessarily resulted in the proliferation of multiethnic churches that encompass this diversity. Recent studies point toward the stubbornness of ethnic homogeneity in the local church. In *United by Faith*, the authors assert that the percentage of Christian congregations that are considered racially mixed (no one racial group being more than 80 percent of the congregation) is about 5 ½ percent.[7] Often the lack of diversity in congregations is attributed to the lack of diversity in neighborhoods. Michael Emerson reveals, however, that "the vast majority of congregations are substantially less racially diverse than the neighborhoods in which they reside."[8]

Emerson uses two different units of measurement on the level of integration in the church. The general heterogeneity index reveals that "the average (mean) congregational diversity in the United States is merely

.08, while the mean racial diversity of public schools in the United States is .48—suggesting that public schools . . . are six times more racially diverse than are religious congregations." The dissimilarity index showed that "cities with indexes of dissimilarity greater than .60 are considered highly segregated. . . . The value for Catholicism is .81; for mainline Protestantism, .85; and for conservative Protestantism, .91. These figures indicate hyper-segregation."[9] These two measurements reveal that American churches are significantly more segregated than American society, even more segregated than schools and neighborhoods.

In a particular urban neighborhood, the local school has students from over seventy different nationalities that speak fifty different languages. The school represents the increasing diversity of the US population. However, the local church just down the block from the school has an overwhelmingly white majority with minimal reflection of the diversity in the neighborhood. While there is diversity in the larger US culture and there is macrodiversity in the American church, that diversity has not been as evident in the local church that remains highly segregated. In other words, 11 a.m. Sunday morning remains the most segregated hour in America.

> **THE HOMOGENOUS Unit Principle (HUP)**
> **gave the church permission to operate**
> **under *de facto* segregation.**

The persistence of segregation in the US church can be traced in part to the broad influence of the Church Growth Movement (CGM) among American evangelicals in the latter part of the twentieth century.[10] Originally intended by its progenitor, Donald McGavran, to support the efforts of overseas missionaries, CGM principles were eventually modified by C. Peter Wagner at Fuller Theological for US church leaders. CGM principles quickly became popularized through key evangelical pastors.

One of the key tenets of CGM is the Homogenous Unit Principle (HUP), which claimed that it is easier to convert individuals and grow churches with demographically (i.e., racially) similar people.[11] The HUP arises from the sociological concept of homophily. The homophily principle states that "contact between similar people occurs at a higher rate than among dissimilar people."[12] CGM advances the numerical growth as a high priority for the church. Growth occurs most easily, therefore, when you reach out to people who are in your current network of relationships that tend to fall along homogenous clusters. Relationships form the basis of evangelism and church growth and if our relationships are homogenous, our churches will be as well.

Racial segregation, therefore, becomes normalized. It is perfectly normal to want to invite your friends to church, and if your friends are of the same race, ethnicity, and social class, then your church begins to grow along homogenous lines. Racial segregation is promoted under the guise of church growth principles. A prominent book on church growth techniques promotes the concept that a church should identify a target audience to grow the church. The book proceeds to depict the ideal candidate to join the church as a middle-aged white male with a polo shirt and khaki pants. When I see that picture and read the "type" of person that the church wants to reach, I can easily deduce that I am not welcome at that church.

The rise of the HUP as a common ecclesial practice occurred when most neighborhoods (and many of the institutions) in the United States remained segregated. The HUP reflected the social reality of staunch segregation in our society. In the twenty-first century, there exists greater diversity in our local neighborhoods and in the larger context of the church in the United States. Yet, the church remains extremely segregated. This high level of segregation reveals the ingrained nature of racialized church practices. The HUP gave the church permission to operate under *de facto* segregation. The church could define what kinds of people are "like us" and choose to tailor ministry to suit those "like us."

Under the guise of the HUP, the US church effectively deferred the issue of racial integration and racial justice. Segregation in the church could be justified for the sake of evangelization and church growth. However, the sociological motivation for this prioritization diminished the theological understanding of God's intention for His church. In contrast to the HUP, God's intention for the church was for a multiethnic, racially diverse, and racially reconciled community. The Scriptures testify to this intention. As the church, we need to engage this biblical vision that embraces the diversity in the church rather than operate from a pragmatism that reinforces a dysfunctional social reality.

RECOVERING A BIBLICAL VIEW OF CHURCH

In Micah 4, we are introduced to a vision of God's kingdom that encompasses the diversity of humanity. Micah 4:1–2 (NIV)says: *In the last days the mountain of the LORD's temple will be established as chief among the mountains; it will be raised above the hills, and peoples will stream to it. Many nations will come and say, "Come, let us go up to the mountain of the LORD, to the house of the God of Jacob. He will teach us his ways, so that we may walk in his paths." The law will go out from Zion, the word of the LORD from Jerusalem.* Micah 4 presents the biblical promise of an ethnically diverse community that offers united worship to God.

God's intention for diversity begins with the very beginning of human history in Genesis. All of humanity is created in the image of God. We were created with the intention of reflecting unity in YHWH in the midst of diversity. Being created male and female reflects the necessity of community and human interdependence in order to fully reflect the image of God. We need each other to reflect the image of God.

Furthermore, the image of God allows us to reflect God's creativity. "The image of God leads to the spiritual capacity of humanity to hold an affirming and positive position in creation order. That position results in a responsibility to further the creative work of God."[13] That effort finds expression in the formation of culture. Culture arises from the impulse of those made in God's image to express creativity. However, human sinfulness enters the equation leading to separation between humanity, including the separation of humanity at the Tower of Babel. The curse enacted at the Tower of Babel was not the creation of different cultures but the dividing walls of hostility that developed between different cultures. Sin created discord where there should have been unity across the differences. The curse of segregation emerged from the sinful rebellion at the Tower of Babel.

The image in Micah 4 is the reversal of the image in Genesis 11 at the Tower of Babel. In contrast to dispersion from the human construction of the tower, Micah 4 reveals that *people stream to the mountain of the LORD, many nations long to go to the mountain of the LORD.* Where once people were separated and divided, now people are united and gathered before God. Instead of a tower built as a monument to humanity that leads to separation, the mountain of YHWH established by the Lord provides the restoration of human community. Micah 4 promises the reverse of the curse of Babel.

As a child growing up in a Korean American church, I was blessed to encounter Christians from the majority culture. Books, Christian resources, and guest speakers sharing from the majority culture perspective contributed to my spiritual formation. Later in life, as a college student, seminary student, and as a young church planter, I was blessed by the mentorship and influence of African American, Latino/a, and Native American Christians who spoke truth into my life. To not encounter and learn from different communities would have resulted in a significant spiritual and intellectual void in my life. Learning across cultural and racial boundaries has allowed me to reverse that potential curse and to find great joy and growth in cross-cultural relationships. Micah 4 reminds me that I am no longer under the curse of the Tower of Babel, living under an oppressive system of segregation that separates me from my fellow believer because of racial and ethnic differences. Instead, I have the privilege of engaging across the dividing walls of hostility and finding a spiritual vibrancy in a restored Christian community.

YHWH longs to establish His people as *chief among the mountains . . . raised above the hills.* God's longing is to set His people on a high place as a standard of community. This community will be a multiethnic gathering place of reconciliation. Many peoples and nations will stream to the church, reversing the curse and setting right what human sin has destroyed. Unfortunately, the church in the United States falls short of the image of Micah 4. While many nations are present in the macro makeup of the American church, the deeper reconciliation between the different races has remained elusive. Micah 4 reveals God's longing for His people to be presented as a multiethnic community; but as outlined above, that diverse community is far from the reality in our local church, and segregation remains a key characteristic of the church in the United States.

Micah 4 raises the promise of a racially reconciled multiethnic community and also offers how this community comes to pass. Micah 4:3 (NIV) presents a picture of peace in a community comprised of formerly hostile people with the promise that *they will beat their swords into plowshares and their spears into pruning hooks. Nation will not take up sword against nation, nor will they train for war anymore.* Warfare and conflict between the peoples comes to an end and peace is introduced. The dividing walls of hostility will fall and there will be no more need for battle.

If we long to enter into this time of cessation of hostility, is there a willingness to put down the sword that is held aloft over the other? Is there a willingness to enter into a state of powerlessness and defenselessness that will result when agrarian tools replace weapons of power? Will the majority culture be willing to yield the sword that determines theological rightness of minority cultures? Will the majority culture be willing to yield the sword that determines ecclesial appropriateness for other cultures? Will the dominant culture be willing to place themselves in a position of learning rather than a position of teaching?

PART OF LAYING down the sword implies the willingness to receive correction, rebuke, and guidance from those who are not of the same ethnicity and race.

Almost every person of color in evangelical circles has had a white mentor, supervisor, pastor, professor, or other person of authority over them. In contrast, white evangelicals can advance through a successful ministry career without a single nonwhite person of influence over their lives. Part of laying down the sword implies the willingness to receive correction, rebuke, and guidance from those who are not of the same ethnicity and race. The willingness to submit to the authority of the other reveals the willingness to lay down the sword.

The laying down of the sword implies a willingness to lay down power for the sake of unity among God's people. The reversal of the curse pulls us out of the place of comfort often associated with separation and segregation. The hostility and the dysfunctional power structure that can develop from segregation can be the sword that is laid down in order to move toward a place of unity and cooperation. The existing systems of war, abusive use of power, and hostility are replaced with common worship and an establishment of a safe place without fear for each person.

Micah 4:4 (NIV) presents an image of a safe place for God's people: *Every man will sit under his own vine and under his own fig tree, and no one will make them afraid, for the LORD Almighty has spoken.* This sense of security is offered to all members of the community, not merely to those who hold power and privilege. It is not a place of paternalism and not a place of being a stranger to one another. Instead, it is a place where you do not fear that you will be told that you do not belong, you do not fit in, and that you will always be an outsider. Micah 4 not only calls us to the high calling of a racially reconciled, multiethnic community, but it also calls us to lay down our swords of power and hostility to create a community where the historically marginalized find a safe haven.

For many ethnic minorities, immigrant and ethnic specific churches have served as safe places. As a Korean American, my name is often mispronounced in multiethnic settings. In the Korean church, my "funny-sounding" name is normal. In a multiethnic church setting, bringing *kimchi* to a potluck could be a major social *faux pas*. I need to explain to the uninitiated that *kimchi* is not some sort of toxic waste and that it will not eat away your insides. But in a Korean church, the whole building can smell of *kimchi* and nobody minds. The immigrant church can be a refuge and a safe place.

Moving into a multiethnic, multicultural setting can also prove to be an unsafe space. Minorities may encounter stereotypes, caricatures, and an exoticizing of nonwhite cultures in web pages, books, children's curriculum, skits, conferences, even YouTube clips, Facebook posts, and twitter feeds from Christian leaders. The larger evangelical culture steeped in Western white cultural captivity is not necessarily a safe place for evangelicals of color. A white student at an evangelical seminary is virtually assured that the overwhelming majority of his/

her instructors will be of the same ethnicity. There is no such assurance for an ethnic minority student that any instructor will be of his/her ethnicity. These realities can create unsafe spaces.

The description of a multiethnic community in Micah 4 calls for the creation of safe places for all participants in the worship of YHWH. What authority is being yielded, what power is being shared, and what swords are being laid down? Through these acts, unsafe places can become safe spaces. I have deeply appreciated the willingness by white evangelicals who have mis-stepped in these areas to offer public apologies, seek ways to understand, and offer constructive correctives. LifeWay,[14] Zondervan,[15] and the Exponential Conference are specific examples of evangelical institutions that have offered public apologies after offending a minority community. These actions shift unsafe spaces into safe spaces.

The prophecy of Micah 4 finds the beginning of fulfillment in the book of Acts. Acts 2 provides a glimpse of God's restoration and the reversing of the curse. Different people groups are gathered together in a reversal of Genesis 11, even to the point of one unifying language. The church that is birthed in Acts 2 is now a reflection of the unity promised in Micah 4 with the sharing of resources and a common worship life.

The New Testament Epistles continue this testimony as God's people are challenged to live a life worthy of the calling and to tear down the dividing walls of hostility. The Epistles provide guidelines on how to live out the multiethnic vision of Micah and the glimpse of the multiethnic future in the book of Acts. This vision culminates in the future hope of Revelation 7:9 (NIV), where we are presented with the image of *a great multitude that no one could count, from every nation, tribe, people and language standing before the throne and in front of the Lamb.* The challenge of the multiethnic church in the United States today is how we may live in the tension of the promise of a multiethnic community in Micah 4, the inauguration of the multiethnic community in Acts 2, the challenge to live into the multiethnic community in the New Testament Epistles, and the future consummation of that community in Revelation 7:9 contrasted with the reality of a segregated church in the United States.

My denomination, the Evangelical Covenant Church, began as part of the Swedish Free Church movement that immigrated to the United States. There is a deeply rooted Swedish immigrant narrative in the denomination. In the last few decades, the Covenant has moved toward a broader engagement with multiethnic ministry. The Covenant is arguably one of the most successful denominations to transition from an ethnic specific evangelical institution to a genuinely multiethnic denomination. Part of the success is due to the establishment of a fivefold test to gauge progress toward ethnic diversity. The five categories are 1) Population, 2) Participation, 3) Power, 4) Pacesetting, and 5) Purposeful Narrative.

Many churches and denominations are satisfied with a diverse population and multiethnic participation. Having different faces in the congregation is considered to be enough progress. But power must be shared, the outsiders must now become the pacesetters, and the historical narrative of the previously marginalized now becomes essential to the ongoing narrative of the community. The Evangelical Covenant Church recognized that in order to be an intentional and authentic multiethnic community, power must be laid down and a safe space must be created for those who have previously been marginalized. Micah 4 presents the biblical challenge to move toward this type of community.

LETTER FROM A BIRMINGHAM JAIL

Despite the gulf of time between the historic letter and our current reality, Dr. King offers wisdom and insight relevant for today. King dealt with extreme levels of segregation in American society enforced by the state. The twenty-first-century church in the United States deals with extreme levels of segregation brought about by deeply engrained ecclesial practices. Today, more than ever, confronted with a multi-ethnic social reality and a church culture that does not match that reality, we need to heed the prophetic words of Dr. Martin Luther King in his letter from a Birmingham jail.

When addressing the segregated church in the United States and the dearth of multiethnic churches, we must deal with deep rooted injustices. These injustices require confrontation with biblical justice, not moderation. Before moving too quickly to building multiethnic churches, we must address the systems that exist that prevent the work of multiethnic churches. Injustices in the church that led to segregation must be addressed. King made it clear that he had come to Birmingham to address an injustice. "I am in Birmingham because injustice is here." King goes on to assert that "injustice anywhere is a threat to justice everywhere. We are caught in an inescapable network of mutuality, tied in a single garment of destiny."[16]

As multiethnic churches gain greater interest among twenty-first-century evangelicals, two different streams of multiethnic ministry have emerged. The first stream develops multiethnic ministry from a color blind approach. The color blind approach assumes that everybody comes to the table on equal terms. Race and culture are inconsequential and we do not need to deal with our differences and we certainly don't have to deal with our tainted history. Racial and cultural issues only distract us from the real work of the church. The color blind approach may require that participants in multiethnic ministry check their race and culture at the door. It may require that "you get over it" in order to move toward the "real work" of growing the multiethnic church.

The reconciliation approach acknowledges an unjust history. It does not seek to present a church that is merely a show and looks good to others. Instead, the reconciliation approach recognizes that there have been injustices and we must address these injustices. Racial reconciliation and racial justice undergirds rather than distracts from the work of a multiethnic church. The reconciliation approach considers the painful history of ethnic minorities. It refuses to allow historic injustice to go unaddressed.

The reality of a segregated church in the twenty-first century did not emerge without a historical context. Historical racial segregation must be confronted. This segregation is not just rooted in the Jim Crow South but also emerges out of a *de facto* segregation justified by the Church Growth Movement. Establishing a multiethnic church must deal with a long history of segregation. Remembering our difficult history is not an easy task. It is too easy to slip into what is comfortable and to be satisfied with the status quo.

The call from Dr. King and from Scripture is to address injustice with biblical justice. The church cannot gloss over historical injustice and ongoing expressions of injustice. Current expressions of the church often seek easy answers. We jump to multiethnic ministry without the prerequisite work of racial reconciliation and racial justice. Minority voices have been silenced by the church. The hard work of racial justice may necessitate the elevation of minority voices in our expression of multiethnic ministry. These voices have been silenced in an act of injustice. That injustice must be addressed. A color blind approach reflects moderation efforts that may curtail works of justice. Multiethnic churches require justice, not moderation.

The work of the multiethnic church does not shy away from places of tension. Dr. King speaks of a creative tension that leads to a necessary confrontation with the issue of injustice. King states: "I am not afraid of the word 'tension.'" Racial justice required for the work of multiethnic ministry can lead to tension and discomfort. The necessary tension of multiethnic ministry may cause a disruption in the status quo. King recognizes that those who currently hold the power and possess privilege will be "dedicated to the task of maintaining the status quo. . . . it is so often the arch supporter of the status quo." King notes that "privileged groups seldom give up their privileges voluntarily."

The cost of an authentic and biblical multiethnic ministry requires the sacrifice of the dominant culture. Dr. King confronts the dominant culture, particularly moderate whites who are unwilling to yield power for the sake of others. King expressed his disappointment in this portion of his letter:

> I have been gravely disappointed with the white moderate. I have almost reached the regrettable conclusion that the Negro's great stumbling block in the stride toward freedom is not the White Citizens Counciler or the Ku Klux Klanner but the white moderate who is more devoted to order than to justice; who prefers a negative peace which is the absence of tension to a positive peace which is the presence of justice.[17]

This disappointment is not merely expressed toward moderate whites in the context of American society but particularly in the context of the church. King states: "I have been disappointed with the white church and its leadership. . . . I felt that the white ministers, priests, and rabbis of the South would be some of our strongest allies. Instead, some few have been outright opponents, refusing to understand the freedom movement and misrepresenting its leaders; all too many others have been more cautious than courageous and have remained silent behind the anesthetizing security of stained-glass windows. . . . I have watched white churches stand on the sidelines and merely mouth pious irrelevancies and sanctimonious trivialities."[18]

Racial justice is hard work. King's concern reflects the reality that if we do not pursue biblical justice, we are often reinforcing the status quo that perpetuates justice. The biblical call for multiethnic ministry requires the hard work of justice pursuit. It requires the laying down of power that has previously been distributed in an unjust manner. This call requires the radical effort to deal with historical injustice, even if it costs those who have benefited from the existing system of power and privilege. In light of demographic changes in US society, will the church in America heed the words of Scripture and lay down power and privilege for the sake of others? The church that God seeks to raise above all other high places has this moment in history to fulfill the challenge of Dr. King and the challenge of Micah 4 to live into the high calling of being a truly reconciled church.

CONTRIBUTOR BIOGRAPHIES

JOHN BRYSON: John is a founder, pastor, and elder of Fellowship Memphis, a multicultural church ministering in Memphis, Tennessee. John also serves on the board of Acts29 and as a church planting coach with Fellowship Associates. He has a doctorate in leadership from Gordon-Conwell Theological Seminary, along with degrees from Dallas Seminary (MABS), the University of North Texas (MBA), and Asbury College (B.A.). John is the author and presenter of *College Ready* and lead writer and copresenter of a curriculum entitled *33 The Series* with Authentic Manhood. John and Beth were married in 1994 and are the proud parents of Brooke, Beck, Bo, Boss, and Blair. He was born and raised in Harlan, Kentucky, spent eleven years in Denton, Texas, and has lived in Memphis since 2003.

MATT CHANDLER: Matt Chandler serves as lead pastor of teaching at the Village Church in the Dallas/Fort Worth metroplex. The church has witnessed a tremendous response, growing from 160 people to over 11,000 with campuses in Flower Mound, Dallas, Denton, and Fort Worth. He serves as president of Acts 29, a worldwide church planting organization. Over the last ten years, Acts 29 has emerged from a small band of brothers to nearly five hundred churches in the United States and around the world. Beyond speaking at conferences throughout the world, Matt has also written three books, *The Explicit Gospel*, published in April 2012, *Creature of the Word*, released in October 2012, and *To Live Is Christ, To Die Is Gain*, released in September 2013. His greatest joy outside of Jesus is being married to Lauren and being a dad to their three children, Audrey, Reid, and Norah.

CHARLIE E. DATES: Charlie Dates is the senior pastor of Progressive Missionary Baptist Church in Chicago, Illinois. In 2011, at age thirty, he became the youngest pastor in Progressive's rich ninety-three-year history. He has a bachelor of arts in speech communication and rhetoric from University of Illinois at Urbana-Champaign, master of divinity degree from Trinity Evangelical Divinity School in Deerfield, Illinois, and is currently earning a Ph.D. in historical theology at Trinity Evangelical Divinity School. In addition to his pastoral duties, Charlie serves as an adjunct professor at the Moody Bible Institute and on the community advisory board for the Chicago Fire Department. He is married to Kirstie Dates and is the proud father of their children, Charlie Edward Dates II and Claire Elisabeth Dates.

BRYAN LORITTS: Bryan is the lead pastor of Fellowship Memphis Church, a multiethnic church ministering to the urban Memphis community. Bryan has a master's degree in theology and is currently working on his PhD. In addition to serving the community of Memphis, Bryan's ministry takes him across the country as he speaks to thousands annually at churches, conferences, and retreats. He is the author of *God on Paper* and *A Cross Shaped Gospel*. He is also a contributing author for *Great Preaching* and was recently voted as one of the top thirty emerging Christian leaders in the country by *Outreach* magazine. He serves on the board of trustees at Biola University. Bryan is married to Korie, and is the father of three sons: Quentin, Myles, and Jaden. You can follow Bryan on twitter: @bcloritts.

CRAWFORD LORITTS: Crawford Loritts is the senior pastor of Fellowship Bible Church in Atlanta. He holds a bachelor of science degree from Philadelphia Biblical University, a doctor of divinity from Biola University, and a doctor of sacred theology from Philadelphia Biblical University. He is a visiting professor at Trinity Evangelical

Divinity School; author of seven books, *Leadership as an Identity*, *A Passionate Commitment*, *Never Walk Away*, *Make It Home Before Dark*, *Lessons from a Life Coach*, *Developing Character in Your Child* (coauthored with his wife, Karen), and *For a Time We Cannot See*; and the host of the daily radio program *Living a Legacy*. He and his wife, Karen, speak at numerous marriage and family conferences and are the proud parents of Bryan, Heather, Bryndan, and Holly.

JOHN M. PERKINS: In 1989, John Perkins called together a group of Christian leaders from across America that was bonded by one significant commitment—expressing the love of Christ in America's poor communities, not at arm's length but at the grassroots level. An association was formed and the Christian Community Development Association (CCDA) held its first annual conference in Chicago in 1989. CCDA has grown from thirty-seven founding members to sixty-eight hundred individuals and six hundred churches, ministries, institutions, and businesses in more than one hundred cities and townships across the country. Despite being a third-grade dropout, Perkins has been recognized for his work with eleven honorary doctorates from colleges and universities across the country and two universities have established John Perkins centers. He is an international speaker and teacher on racial reconciliation, leadership, and the philosophy of ministry known as Christian Community Development.

JOHN PIPER: John Piper is founder and teacher of desiringGod. org and chancellor of Bethlehem College and Seminary. For thirty-three years, he served as senior pastor at Bethlehem Baptist Church, Minneapolis, Minnesota. He grew up in Greenville, South Carolina, and studied at Wheaton College, Fuller Theological Seminary (B.D.), and the University of Munich (Th.D.). For six years, he taught biblical studies at Bethel College in St. Paul, Minnesota, and in 1980 accepted the call to serve as pastor at Bethlehem. John is the author of more than fifty books; and more than thirty years of his preaching and teaching is available free at desiringGod.org. John and his wife, Noel, have four sons, one daughter, and twelve grandchildren.

SOONG-CHAN RAH: Soong-Chan Rah is the Milton B. Engebretson Associate Professor of Church Growth and Evangelism at North Park Theological Seminary in Chicago, Illinois; the author of *The Next Evangelicalism: Freeing the Church from Western Cultural Captivity* (IVP Books, 2009) and *Many Colors: Cultural Intelligence for the Changing Church* (Moody Publishers, 2010); and coeditor of *Honoring the Generations: Learning with Asian North American Congregations* (Judson Press, 2012). He was founding pastor of Cambridge Community Fellowship Church, a multiethnic, urban ministry focused church committed to living out the values of racial reconciliation and social justice in the urban context. He studied at Columbia University (B.A.); Gordon-Conwell Theological Seminary (M.Div., D. Min.); Harvard University (Th.M.), and Duke University (currently working toward his Th.D.). He and his wife, Sue, have two children (Annah and Elijah) and reside in Chicago.

ALBERT TATE: Albert Tate is lead pastor of Fellowship in Monrovia, California. From Sweet Home Church of Christ Holiness in Mississippi to Lake Avenue Church in California, Albert brings many years of ministry experience and has served in a variety of strategic leadership positions. He is a gifted and dynamic communicator, passionate about living in community, a lover of his family, and believes the local church is God's greatest hope for the world. Albert presents the gospel to students across the country in both academic and retreat settings, combining humor and storytelling of God's amazing grace and love. His unique and passionate style from the pulpit combines inspiration and challenge, laughter and tears, as people are engaged at their core. He cherishes his wife, LaRosa, who is God's gift of amazing grace in his life—and their three darling young children, Zoe, Bethany, and Isaac.

SANDERS L. WILLSON: Sanders L. (Sandy) Willson has been the senior minister of Second Presbyterian Church, Memphis, Tennessee, since 1995. He serves on the Gospel Coalition board and on the board of reference for Union University and Reformed Theological Seminary. Sandy's Sunday morning messages are broadcast on WREG TV (CBS affiliate); he also teaches five hundred men at AMEN Bible Study every Thursday at 6:30 a.m. Sandy received a B.S. from the University of Virginia (1973), a M.Div. from Gordon-Conwell Theological Seminary (1982), and a D.D. from Crichton College in Memphis, Tennessee (2001). He and his wife, Allison, are grateful for five children, three daughters-in-law, a son-in-law, and seven grandchildren.

ACKNOWLEDGMENTS

LETTERS TO A BIRMINGHAM JAIL has been in my soul for years, at least conceptually, but it wasn't until I had a conversation with Pastor Albert Tate that the idea began to take shape. So a huge debt of gratitude is owed to my son in the ministry and friend, Albert.

I felt deeply that a black man writing yet another book on race and its tributary themes was not going to accomplish what I at least had envisioned for this project; there needed to be a multiethnic cohort of Jesus loving authors who embodied and wrote in such a way that the broader culture was jolted out of her slumber. So phone calls were placed to men of various ages and ethnicities. As I shared the vision for this book with them, there was an overwhelming sense of both excitement and agreement. These men represent an undying commitment to our Lord and Savior, Jesus Christ, coupled with a courageous striving to see Christ-exalting diversity. Crawford Loritts, John Piper, Soong-Chan Rah, Charlie Dates, Sandy Willson, John Bryson, John Perkins, Albert Tate, and Matt Chandler, I am grateful for not just the words you put forth in this book but the life that you live.

As this project was coming to a close, I found myself engaged in conversation with Dr. Mark Noll at a conference we were presenting on the campus of Wheaton College. For years I had run to his books finding great inspiration, and so I asked him to write the foreword, and he graciously agreed. Thank you, Dr. Noll.

Danielle Ridley, my assistant, played a key role in corresponding with the authors and corralling all of the endorsements. She is an exceptional colaborer with me not just in this venture but in the ministry

God has entrusted to me. My literary agent, Andrew Wolgemuth, was a sounding board for the essays, providing helpful feedback. Ours has been a partnership for which I hope will last a long time. Roslyn Jordan at Moody Publishers, along with her team, offered valuable suggestions, especially when it came to the unity of this book. Their insights took what I consider to be a great project into the stratosphere. Thank you.

My bride, Korie, spent hours reading the manuscript. I can always lean on her for support, but also for gracious truth. I am blessed beyond measure to have journeyed with her thus far, and by God's grace the romantic trip will continue "until death do us part." Thank you, sweetheart.

It was fun to serve as "the boss" of my father, Crawford Loritts, in this effort. As you can imagine my theology of ethnicity was foundationally shaped at 551 Mary Erna Drive, there in Fairburn, Georgia, where I grew up. His life inspired me to run after Christ-exalting diversity. Thanks, Dad.

NOTES

Introduction

1. Diane McWhorter, *Carry Me Home: Birmingham, Alabama, The Climactic Battle of the Civil Rights Revolution* (New York: Simon and Schuster, 2001), 337.

Chapter 1: Why We Can't Wait for Economic Justice

1. Clara Tear Williams, "Satisfied," 1875.

Chapter 2: Waiting for and Hastening the Day of Multiethnic Beauty

1. Stephen B. Oates, *Let the Trumpet Sound* (New York: A Mentor Book, 1982), 222.

2. Simon & Garfunkel, "I Am a Rock," Copyright ©1965, Sony Music Entertainment.

3. Guy Gugliotta, "New Estimate Raises Civil War Death Toll," *New York Times: Science,* 12 Apr. 2012, http://www.nytimes.com/2012/04/03/science/civil-war-toll-up-by-20-percent-in-new-estimate.html?pagewanted=all&_r=0 (cited on 10-31-2013).

4. Tashai Tafari, "The Rise and Fall of Jim Crow," Public Broadcasting Station Online, http://www.pbs.org/wnet/jimcrow/struggle_congress.html (cited 10-31-2013).

5. Carl Chancellor, "After Civil War, Blacks Fought for Rights for 100 Years," *USA Today*, 17 May 2011, http://usatoday30.usatoday.com/news/nation/2011-04-11-civil-war-civil-rights_N.htm (cited 10-31-2013). "The origin of the phrase 'Jim Crow' has often been attributed to 'Jump Jim Crow,' a song-and-dance caricature of blacks performed by white actor Thomas Rice in blackface which first surfaced in 1832 and was used to satirize Andrew Jackson's populist policies. As a result of Rice's fame, 'Jim Crow' had become a pejorative expression meaning 'Negro' by 1838. When southern legislatures passed laws of racial segregation—directed against blacks—at the end of the 19th century, these became known as Jim Crow laws." http://en.wikipedia.org/wiki/Jim_crow (cited 10-31-2013).

6. Chancellor, "After Civil War, Blacks Fought for Rights for 100 Years."

7. Marshall Frady, *Jesse: The Life and Pilgrimage of Jesse Jackson* (New York: Simon and Schuster, 2006), 82.

8. John Piper, *Bloodlines: Race, Cross, and the Christian* (Wheaton: Crossway Books, 2011). Some of the wording in this chapter is brought over from this book.

9. Stephen B. Oates, *Let the Trumpet Sound* (New York: A Mentor Book, 1982), 210.

10. "A Call for Unity," *Birmingham News*, April 12, 1963, http://en.wikipedia.org/wiki/A_Call_For_Unity (cited 12-1-2013).

11. Martin Luther King Jr., "Letter from a Birmingham Jail," http://www.africa.upenn.edu/Articles_Gen/Letter_Birmingham.html.

12. Ibid.

13. Ibid.

14. Bob Dylan, "Blowing in the Wind," Copyright © 1962 by Warner Bros. Inc.; renewed 1990 by Special Rider Music. http://www.bobdylan.com/us/songs/blowin-wind (cited 10-31-2013).

15. Martin Luther King Jr, "Letter from a Birmingham Jail," http://www.africa.upenn.edu/Articles_Gen/Letter_Birmingham.html.

16. Carl Ellis Jr., *Free at Last: The Gospel in the African-American Experience* (Downers Grove, IL: InterVarsity Press, 1996), 23.

17. Ibid., 214. The term is carefully chosen and defined by Carl Ellis in *Free at Last*, 214, "This ugly term is most fitting because of its ugliness, to refer to the negative or unchristian religious practices expressed in the language of Christianity . . ."

18. Ibid., 154.

19. For one small example how we tried to obey this at Bethlehem Baptist Church, see the short article, "How and Why Bethlehem Pursues Ethnic Diversity," at http://www.desiringgod.org/resource-library/taste-see-articles/how-and-why-bethlehem-pursues-ethnic-diversity/print?lang=en.

Chapter 5: Why We Can't Wait for the Multiethnic Church

1. Taylor Branch, *Parting the Waters* (New York: Simon and Shuster, 1988), 207.

Chapter 6: Why Traditional Suburban Churches Can't Wait

1. Michael Emerson and Christian Smith, *Divided by Faith: Evangelical Religion and the Problem of Race in America* (New York: Oxford University Press, 2000), 11–14.

2. Ibid.

3. Martin Luther King Jr., "Letter from a Birmingham City Jail," in James M. Washington, ed., *Testament of Hope* (San Francisco: Harper, 1986), 289–302.

4. Local Rhodes College professor Dr. Stephen Haynes has documented these events in his *The Last Segregated Hour* (New York: Oxford Press), 2012.

5. See "Statement of Intention Regarding Race Relations at Second Presbyterian Church," at www.2pc.org.

6. Martin Luther King Jr., "Non Violence and Racial Justice," in James M. Washington, ed., *A Testament of Hope* (San Francisco: Harper, 1986), 9.

Chapter 8: Why We Can't Wait for Christ-Exalting Diversity

1. According to Luke 1:3, Luke's gospel was commissioned by and written to the God-lover, Theophilus. How ironic it is that the white power structure of Birmingham was so steeply entrenched in Southern church ground.

2. King did not prefer the language of black church and white church. In chapter 6 of his book *Strength to Love*, he wrote "I say so-called Negro church because ideally there can be no Negro or white church. It is to their everlasting shame that white Christians developed a system of racial segregation within the church, and inflicted so many indignities upon its Negro worshippers that they had to organize their own churches."

3. Flip Shulke and Penelope McPhee, *King Remembered* (New York: Pocket Books, 1986), 118.

4. Mervyn A. Warren, *King Came Preaching: The Pulpit Power of Dr. Martin Luther King Jr.* (Downers Grove, IL: InterVarsity Academic Press, 2001).

5. Harold W. Hoehner, *Ephesians: An Exegetical Commentary* (Ada, MI: Baker Academic, 2002).

6. *Dictionary of Paul and His Letters* (Downers Grove, IL: InterVarsity Press). This dictionary is one of the most helpful sources toward understanding the semantic domain of the Greek word "reconciliation" and Paul's use of it. Reconciliation in Pauline writings consists of both making peace and killing hostility. It is a defining and final verdict on the evil compositions of church divisions.

7. This is the controlling subject of the long sentence that makes up Ephesians 2:14–16.

8. Martin L. King Jr., "Letter from a Birmingham Jail 1963," in *Testament of Hope* (New York: Harper Collins, 1986), 299.

9. Ibid., 491–92.

10. Ibid., 495.

11. Ibid., 296.

12. Ibid., 300.

Chapter 9: The Time Is Now for Multiethnic Churches and Movements

1. Martin Luther King Jr., "Letter from a Birmingham Jail," http://www.africa. upenn.edu/Articles_Gen/Letter_Birmingham.html.

2. Matt Chandler, Eric Geiger, Josh Patterson, *Creature of the Word: The Jesus Centered Church* (Nashville: B&H Books, 2012).

3. Cornelius Plantinga, *Engaging God's World: A Christian Vision of Faith, Learning and Living* (Grand Rapids: Eerdmans, 2002).

4. Matt Perman, "What Is the Doctrine of the Trinity?" http://www.desiringgod. org/resource-library/articles/what-is-the-doctrine-of-the-trinity.

5. Adam Lancaster, *The Culture-Sharing Church*, http://www.thevillagechurch. net/the-village-blog/author/adam-lancaster/.

6. Chandler, Geiger, and Patterson, *Creature of the Word*.

7. John Piper, http://www.desiringgod.org/resource-library/taste-see-articles/ how-and-why-bethlehem-pursues-ethnic-diversity.

Chapter 10: A More Biblical Sunday Morning

1. Philip Jenkins. *The New Faces of Christianity: Believing the Bible in the Global South* (New York: Oxford University Press, 2006), 9.

2. Curtis J. Evans, "White Evangelical Protestants Responses to the Civil Rights Movement" *Harvard Theological Review* 102:2 (2009): 246–47.

3. Jennifer M. Ortman and Christine E. Guarneri, "United States Population Projections: 2000 to 2050," at http://www.census.gov/population/www/projections/analytical-document09.pdf.

4. R. Stephen Warner, "Religion and New (Post-1965) Immigrants," *American Studies* 41(2/3): 271.

5. R. Stephen Warner, "Coming to America," *Christian Century* 121(3): 20. See also R. Stephen Warner and Judith G. Wittner, eds., *Gatherings in Diaspora* (Philadelphia: Temple University Press, 1998).

6. Mark Chaves, *Continuity and Change* (Princeton, NJ: Princeton University Press, 2011), 24. See also Elaine Ecklund, *Korean American Evangelicals* (New York: Oxford University Press, 2006), and Ana Maria Diaz-Stevens and Anthony M. Stevens-Arroyo, *Recognizing the Latino Resurgence in U.S. Religion* (Boulder, CO: Westview Press, 1998).

7. Curtiss DeYoung, Michael Emerson, George Yancey, and Karen Chai Kim, *United by Faith* (New York: Oxford University Press, 2003), 2. See also Michael Emerson with Rodney Woo, *People of the Dream* (Princeton, NJ: Princeton University Press, 2006) where Emerson asserts that "the number of stable racially mixed congregations is undoubtedly lower than the 7 percent estimated" (36–37).

8. Emerson with Woo, *People of the Dream*, 43–44.

9. Ibid., 37, 40–41.

10. See Gary McIntosh, *Evaluating the Church Growth Movement* (Grand Rapids: Zondervan, 2004), Donald McGavran, *Understanding Church Growth* (Grand Rapids: Eerdmans, 1970); and C. Peter Wagner, *Your Church Can Grow* (Ventura, CA: Regal Books, 1983).

11. See C. Peter Wagner, *Our Kind of People* (Atlanta: John Knox, 1979). The value of numerical growth was seen as more critical than the value of racial reconciliation. See Rah, *The Next Evangelicalism* (Downers Grove, IL: IVP Books, 2009), 91–107 for a more detailed critique.

12. J. M. McPherson and L. Smith-Lovin, "Homophily in Voluntary Organizations," *American Sociological Review* 52:3 (1987): 416.

13. Soong-Chan Rah, *Many Colors: Cultural Intelligence for a Changing Church* (Chicago: Moody Publishers, 2010), 27.

14. Melissa Barnhart, "LifeWay President Apologizes for Decade-Old 'Rickshaw Rally' VBS Curriculum @ Mosaix Conference," *Christian Post: Church and Ministry*, November 7, 2013, www.ChristianPost.com.

15. Sarah Pulliam Bailey, "Zondervan Issues Apology for Publishing 'Deadly Viper,'" *Christianity Today: Gleanings*, November 20, 2009, www.ChristiantyToday.com.

16. Martin Luther King Jr. "Letter from a Birmingham Jail," http://www.africa.upenn.edu/Articles_Gen/Letter_Birmingham.html.

17. Ibid.

18. Ibid.

UNITY. DIVERSITY.
PART OF GOD'S VISION FOR HIS CHURCH

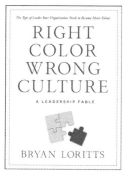

978-0-8024-1173-0

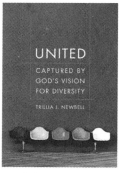

978-0-8024-1014-6

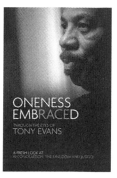

978-0-8024-1790-9

978-0-8024-5048-7

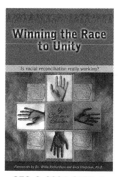

978-0-8024-8159-7

*After this I looked, and there before me was a great multitude
that no one could count, from every nation, tribe, people and
language, standing before the throne and before the Lamb.*

REVELATION 7:9 (NIV)

Bryan Loritts (*Right Color, Wrong Culture*), Trillia
Newbell (*United*), Dr. Tony Evans (*Oneness Embraced*),
Soong Chan Rah (*Many Colors*), and Clarence Schuler
(*Winning the Race to Unity*) . . . voices that remind us
to pursue Christ-exalting unity and diversity as we
seek to love God and our neighbors.

**MOODY
Publishers**™

From the Word to Life

MOODY Radio™

From the Word to Life

Moody Radio produces and delivers compelling programs filled with biblical insights and creative expressions of faith that help you take the next step in your relationship with Christ.

You can hear Moody Radio on 36 stations and more than 1,500 radio outlets across the U.S. and Canada. Or listen on your smartphone with the Moody Radio app!

www.moodyradio.org

urbanpraise

Urban Praise, a commercial-free Moody Radio Internet station, offers a soulful blend of rich gospel and urban music. Energize your faith with artists like Kirk Franklin, Israel Houghton, Shirley Caesar, CeCe Winans, Walter Hawkins, and Lecrae, along with bite-size teaching segments from Tony Evans, Crawford Loritts, Melvin Banks, Beth Moore, and others.

www.urbanpraiseradio.org

MOODY
Radio™
From the Word ***to Life***